What People Are Saying About Joshua Mills and *The Miracle of the Oil*

God continually seeks to encourage and uplift His people. One of the ways He does this is through a fresh anointing of His Holy Spirit to demonstrate His deep love for us and to impart His supernatural power to us. In *The Miracle of the Oil,* Joshua Mills describes how God is sending a miracle anointing to us today in a very special way. As you read this book, receive all the blessings the Lord wants to pour out into your life.

—*Bobby Schuller*
Lead Pastor, Shepherd's Grove, Irvine, CA
Host, *Hour of Power with Bobby Schuller*

Joshua Mills has become a sign and a signet to challenge the body of Christ to walk in the reality of who we are as anointed children of God. In *The Miracle of the Oil,* Joshua's teaching gift is effectively supported by the Scriptures. His testimonies are poignant, and his prayers invite the Holy Spirit to demonstrate His manifest presence to each reader. I have seen him personally manifest miracle oil, along with other signs and wonders, scores of times. While ministering with him, I observed the oil multiply as we anointed hundreds for the impartation. I invite you to personally experience *The Miracle of the Oil* as you soak in the pages of this book. And may you walk forth anointed with fresh oil.

—*Billie Reagan Deck*
Cedars of Lebanon, Inc., Springfield, VA
www.abdeck.net

Miracle oil is a way by which heaven saturates earth with the sweet anointing of God's presence and power. I believe Joshua Mills to be a genuine man of God, one through whom the Lord does extraordinary things. I have personally witnessed supernatural oil appear on Joshua's hands as he's ministered—not from afar, but I have stood right next to him when God's oil began to flow. His testimony is true, and I am a witness to it. I believe that as you read *The Miracle of the Oil*, your boundaries will be enlarged to welcome the amazing God we love and serve.

—*Dale Everett*
Dale Everett Ministries International
www.daleeverett.org

There is no one better qualified to write this book than Joshua Mills. He walks in the miracle of God's anointing, and the glory and oil of the Lord are all over him! The impartation and activation in this book will draw you right in and make you want more. I didn't want to put this book down. *The Miracle of the Oil* holds the tangible presence of God and will empower you with fresh oil from heaven.

—*Kathy DeGraw*
Author, *Mind Battles*, *Unshackled*, and *Prophetic Spiritual Warfare*
Host, Prophetic Spiritual Warfare podcast
kathydegrawministries.org

I love the anointing! Early in my ministry, I studied the composition of the anointing oil in the Old Testament. I've always been fascinated by it, fascinated by anything that releases the power and presence of God, the glory. I also love to read books that give historical accounts of the ways in which God has moved among His people through the years. In *The Miracle of the Oil*, Joshua Mills describes how God's supernatural oil has flowed throughout history and continues to flow into our lives today. With chapters such as "Miracle Power," "Miracle Impartation," and "Miracle Illumination," he shows how God's miracle oil empowers, heals, delivers, and brings joy. This will set you on fire! Joshua's insights on the prophetic meanings of the anointing oil recipe will draw you even closer to God, further transforming your life.

—*Barbara J. Yoder*
Founding and Overseeing Apostle, Shekinah Christian Church, Ann Arbor, MI

DEDICATION

I dedicate this book in honor of my godly parents, Ron and Nancy Mills, and my grandparents on both sides, Rev. Keith and Pearl Mills and Rev. Robert and the late Phyllis Degraw. I want to honor the Lord and walk in His ways, even as you have set a spiritual example for me, Janet, and our children, Lincoln, Liberty, and Legacy. Your love for God and for your family has allowed the miracle oil of blessing to flow throughout our generational lines, and I feel grateful to be part of your legacy. May the oil of anointing continue to flow for many generations to come so that we all may declare, "How great is our God! How great are His miracles!"

"Let each generation tell its children of your mighty acts;
let them proclaim your power."
—Psalm 145:4 (NLT)

JOSHUA MILLS

THE MIRACLE OF THE OIL

Receive the Power of God's Anointing

WHITAKER
HOUSE

Boldface type in the Scripture quotations indicates the author's emphasis. The forms LORD and GOD (in small caps) in Bible quotations represent the Hebrew name for God *Yahweh* (Jehovah), while *Lord* and *God* normally represent the name *Adonai*, in accordance with the Bible version used.

THE MIRACLE OF THE OIL:
Receive the Power of God's Anointing

Joshua Mills
International Glory Ministries
JoshuaMills.com
info@joshuamills.com

ISBN: 978-1-64123-918-9
eBook ISBN: 978-1-64123-919-6
Printed in the United States of America

Whitaker House
1030 Hunt Valley Circle
New Kensington, PA 15068
www.whitakerhouse.com

LC record available at https://lccn.loc.gov/2022021592
LC ebook record available at https://lccn.loc.gov/2022021593

1 2 3 4 5 6 7 8 9 10 11 **W** 29 28 27 26 25 24 23 22

CONTENTS

PART FOUR: STEPPING INTO THE MIRACLE

KEY ANOINTING VERSES

So Jacob got up early in the morning, and took the stone he had put under his head and he set it up as a pillar [that is, a monument to the vision in his dream], and he poured [olive] oil on the top of it [to consecrate it]. (Genesis 28:18)

You shall anoint Aaron and his sons, and consecrate them, that they may serve as priests to Me. (Exodus 30:30)

Then Moses took the anointing oil and anointed the tabernacle and all that was in it, and consecrated them. He sprinkled some of the oil on the altar seven times and anointed the altar and all its utensils, and the basin and its stand, to consecrate them. (Leviticus 8:10–11)

Then he poured some of the anointing oil on Aaron's head and anointed him, to consecrate him. (Leviticus 8:12)

Then Samuel took the flask of oil and poured it on Saul's head, kissed him, and said, "Has the Lord *not anointed you as ruler over His inheritance (Israel)?* (1 Samuel 10:1)

Then Samuel took the horn of oil and anointed David in the presence of his brothers; and the Spirit of the Lord *came*

mightily upon David from that day forward.
(1 Samuel 16:13)

Zadok the priest took a horn of [olive] oil from the [sacred] tent and anointed Solomon. They blew the trumpet, and all the people said, "Long live King Solomon!" (1 Kings 1:39)

I have found David My servant; with My holy oil I have anointed him. (Psalm 89:20)

For when the foolish took their lamps, they did not take any [extra] oil with them, but the wise took flasks of oil along with their lamps. (Matthew 25:3–4)

And they were casting out many demons and were anointing with oil many who were sick, and healing them. (Mark 6:13)

Is anyone among you sick? He must call for the elders (spiritual leaders) of the church and they are to pray over him, anointing him with oil in the name of the Lord; and the prayer of faith will restore the one who is sick, and the Lord will raise him up. (James 5:14–15)

You have an anointing from the Holy One [you have been set apart, specially gifted and prepared by the Holy Spirit], and all of you know [the truth because He teaches us, illuminates our minds, and guards us from error]. (1 John 2:20)

Therefore God, your God, has anointed you with the oil of gladness above your companions. (Hebrews 1:9)

INTRODUCTION: THE SIGN OF THE OIL

"Then I asked the angel, 'What are these two olive trees on each side of the lampstand, and what are the two olive branches that pour out golden oil through two gold tubes?' 'Don't you know?' he asked. 'No, my lord,' I replied. Then he said to me, 'They represent the two anointed ones who stand in the court of the Lord of all the earth.'"
—Zechariah 4:11–14 (NLT)

Something phenomenal is happening in the spirit ream! All over the world, people are experiencing God's supernatural power as He releases a fresh anointing. Men, women, teenagers, boys, and girls—ministers and laypeople alike—are reporting that a heavenly oil is miraculously appearing on their heads, hands, and feet. Some people have even noticed this oil appearing in their homes and churches, dripping down the walls! In my ministry, over the years, I've experienced many wonderful and extraordinary signs and wonders, and this remarkable manifestation is what I refer to as "the miracle of the oil."

I first witnessed this phenomenon during a revival service in Spring Hill, Florida, when I was in my first full-time Christian ministry position. I was leading worship from the keyboard, and I was thrilled to be part of a spiritually hungry community of believers who desired to flow with the rhythmic motions of the Spirit.

In those days, we were experiencing the exhilarating joy of holy laughter and the awe and fear of the Lord that settled upon the congregation as people were caught up in spiritual trances and magnificent heavenly visions. We were also experiencing an increase in healing miracles, and the fragrance of heaven would swirl around us and fill the entire church sanctuary as we lifted our praises to Jesus. God was introducing us to Himself in new and wonderful ways!

In that setting, our hearts were open to receive whatever the Spirit desired to bring to us. Seeing our open hands and open hearts, God began pouring the "miracle oil" of His Spirit upon us. It was precious, it was beautiful, and we knew that we had to cherish it. This was a physical manifestation of God's anointing to heal, restore, and empower His people.

When the physical manifestation of the oil first came to me, it appeared within the creases of my palms. It had a shiny, glistening appearance but was quite subtle—just enough for me to recognize that it was there and God was working. The oil carried a special fragrance from heaven, and I knew that the Lord was bringing me into a fresh anointing. I appreciated what God was doing, and I was thankful for that heaven-sent sign.

Other members of the worship team received this precious anointing at the same time. Some of the singers—Beverly, Nancy, and Evelyn—received the manifestation of miracle oil as they worshipped the Lord. It was flowing from their hands, from their feet, and even from the backs of their necks. For each person, the manifestation was distinct in terms of quantity and where it appeared. It was interesting to me that this sign of God's anointing came on the worshippers first.

Our senior pastor, Rev. Bill Wilson, received this miracle oil flowing from the palms of his hands, too, but rather than a trace amount, the oil was overflowing. God spoke to him, saying he must lay hands on the sick in that moment. I appreciated the fact that Pastor Bill was willing to shift gears in the service, to flow with what God was doing at that time. When the anointing comes, we must be willing to adjust our plans and move into the supernatural flow. It's not for us to determine how God is going to move. In the anointing, we're given the opportunity to move *with* God's plan and power.

We hadn't heard of this manifestation happening before, but we understood that God was orchestrating a supernatural juncture, so we gave ourselves to Him as yielded vessels. When Pastor Bill laid hands on the sick in that service, every person—from one end of the prayer line to the other—reported receiving a healing miracle. Yes, God was definitely at work!

We were wise enough to know that when God sent His sign of the oil, just like the various signs in the Bible, He was sending us a direct message through miraculous means. In the following days, we searched the Scriptures and prayerfully asked the Lord for His revelation concerning "the miracle of the oil," and He faithfully responded by speaking to us through His Word and bringing us insight by the guidance of His Spirit. All the Scriptures we discovered at that time and later times are included in this book. We also discovered that miracle oil had physically appeared for the people of God many times throughout history. This phenomenon wasn't new to God, but it was certainly new to us. The Spirit was speaking in a very clear way.

Several years after this initial manifestation, I was ministering in Rockford, Illinois, at a conference hosted by Rev. Edgar Baillie. Edgar had experienced many wonderful things in the Spirit, but he was best known for the bottle of supernatural oil the Lord had given to him during an occurrence of miraculous provision for his family. He recognized that this special gift was to be used as an anointing oil.

Edgar used that bottle of oil in large miracle gatherings, anointing thousands of people. I saw him use it in many church meetings of various sizes, but no matter how many times he used the miracle oil, the bottle always seemed to refill itself to the top. God was at work.

While I was attending one of Edgar's conferences, in my hotel room, I had a powerful encounter through a night vision. In this vision, the Lord sent an angel to anoint me with oil on my head, hands, and feet. When I awoke, miracle oil was physically flowing from my forehead; it was also overflowing from my hands, and it was pouring from my feet. Instantly, I sat up, and the Spirit spoke to my heart and said, in part, "I have anointed you with fresh oil. When the oil flows, anoint My people for My purposes, and I will do great things." At the voice of the Lord, I trembled and determined to do as He had asked.

Moving from my bed toward the other side of the room, I frantically searched for a container into which I could let the oil flow. Finding nothing suitable, I placed my hands in the bathroom sink after putting the stopper in place, and the oil continued to flow as I worshipped the Lord.

The next morning, some friends came to my hotel room. Upon discovering what the Lord had done, they went out and retrieved bottles that could be used to hold the miracle oil that had flowed during the night. I was thankful for their cooperation and appreciated seeing that they perceived what the Spirit was doing.

I could hardly wait to anoint those who were gathered at the conference because I knew that God was releasing a special blessing. He was doing something new and bringing both me and others into a fresh anointing.

From that day forward, miracle oil has continued to flow from me at various times and places. Each time it happens, I release God's anointing to those who are present and ready to receive. Many times, it happens in a public setting while I am ministering the Word or singing to the Lord in worship. But at other times, the oil begins to manifest during my private hours of prayer and devotion. In our meetings, I have also witnessed countless others receiving this special miracle gift of the oil as they have come to the Lord with open hearts and open hands.

When I studied the Word to learn more about the oil of God, divine revelation began to shine upon my spirit. This truth became deeply hidden within my heart, and I knew that the Spirit was planting something inside me to share at an appointed time. That time has come.

> ***IF OUR HEARTS ARE OPEN, AND WE REMAIN IN A POSTURE OF SURRENDER TO GOD, THE SPIRIT IS ABLE TO TEACH US WHAT WE NEED TO KNOW ABOUT HIS WAYS.***

In this book, I share special testimonies about the miracle oil as well as the things God has revealed to me through His Word concerning His miracle oil that flows in both the natural and spiritual realms. If you desire to receive the power of God's anointing, this book is for you because it is filled to overflowing with an impartation for the supernatural!

The miracle oil can only freely flow for those who are willing to enter into a personal relationship with Jesus Christ. If you've never invited Him into your heart to be your personal Lord and Savior, why not pray this prayer now?

> Jesus, come into my heart. I invite You to be my Lord and Savior. I give You my sin in exchange for the life that only You can give. Thank You for cleansing me with Your blood and giving me a brand-new start. I receive Your gift of salvation. Amen!

If you've just prayed that prayer by faith, you can be sure that Jesus now lives in your heart, and He desires to release the power of His anointing in your life.

I believe that if our hearts are open, and we remain in a posture of surrender to God, the Spirit is able to teach us what we need to know about His ways. Each and every time the Spirit has introduced a new manifestation of His divine presence in my life, He has been faithful to instruct me about it.

My prayer is that this book may become a tool the Spirit will use in *your* life to help *you* receive the power of God's anointing. May you be in awe of God's miraculous works, gleaning many truths from these biblical lessons as you experience for yourself *The Miracle of the Oil*.

1

THE MIRACLE OIL OF GOD

"So that he may make his face glisten with oil."
—Psalm 104:15

I am no stranger to controversy. In our ministry and in our family life, my wife, Janet, and I have personally witnessed the anointing of God moving with such great power that it is literally unexplainable. This can frustrate or upset those who would prefer a more "tamed-down" religious experience. On our first ministry trip to New Zealand, we preached in a town hall, and miracle oil appeared in the room where we were meeting. The oil first appeared at the tops of all four walls, and then it flowed down in large, honey-like, golden drops. This oil was wet to the touch and carried a special fragrance from heaven. It was fresh oil, and those of us who had gathered there received it as a supernatural sign of the Spirit's outpouring.

The host pastors who had invited us to minister in their country were enthusiastic and excited about what God was doing because the presence of the miracle oil was, in part, the answer to their prayers. They had been seeking the Lord for a move of His glory, and it was now beginning to manifest. In each meeting, people were making decisions for Christ, the sick were being healed, deliverance and freedom were being reported, and Jesus was being glorified.

However, not everyone was excited. Many other church leaders in the area had great difficulty accepting what God was doing. They would say things like, "Well, if this is from God, why isn't it happening for me?" or "Where is this specific manifestation mentioned in the Bible?" I don't think those leaders were genuinely looking for answers to their questions. It seemed more likely that they were offended by this unusual manifestation of the Spirit. There's a big difference between proper discernment and personal preference, and we must learn the difference. The miracle oil was quite different from anything they had seen before, and it probably made them feel uncomfortable.

It's also possible they were jealous that others were experiencing something new from the Lord and they weren't. Or maybe they had become settled in their spiritual journeys and didn't want to receive anything new. Either way, this new manifestation presented a problem for them. That problem was *change*.

The miracle oil of God is the oil of change. When God's anointing comes, we are given an opportunity to be changed by Him. If we want to receive His anointing, we must yield to His Spirit and allow Him to do His work. Although, at first, we might not have all the answers, if we seek Him, we can be sure that He will bring the revelation of His purposes that we need. Not only will God begin to give us spiritual insight into what He is doing, but He will allow us to be a part of it!

NATURAL AND SPIRITUAL OIL

To understand how God uses miracle oil in our lives, it is helpful to think about how natural oil is used. In the physical world, we use oil for many purposes:

- For light that shines and illuminates dark places
- For lubrication that enables things to work together smoothly
- For cooking or preparing a nourishing meal
- For ointment that refreshes the skin and improves beauty
- For fuel that empowers and propels us forward
- For energy that keeps us connected, warm, safe, and protected

There is a spiritual parallel to each of the ways in which natural oil is used. The Bible says, *"For ever since the creation of the world His invisible attributes, His eternal power and divine nature, have been clearly seen, being understood through His workmanship [all His creation, the wonderful things that He has made]"* (Romans 1:20). Through the natural realm, we are given insight into the deep spiritual things of God.

Therefore, as we understand the manifestations and functions of oil in the natural world, we may also begin to comprehend God's purposes for miracle oil in our lives. When I speak about "the miracle of the oil," I am not just referring to a particular manifestation but rather to the flowing movement of God's Spirit in us and upon us. He is the Miracle Worker, and He is symbolically represented by the oil. He is the One who gives us "the unction to function."

Today, the Spirit of God is pouring out His supernatural oil all over the world, causing our faces to shine with the light of His goodness, increasing our witness and testimony. God is also making His Word come alive for us in ways we have never comprehended before. He is teaching us how to move in His timing, allowing His Spirit to lead us into *divine revelation* for *divine impartation.*

> ***GOD'S SPIRIT IS THE MIRACLE WORKER, AND HE IS SYMBOLICALLY REPRESENTED BY THE OIL. HE IS THE ONE WHO GIVES US "THE UNCTION TO FUNCTION."***

LIGHT AND ANOINTING

Several years ago, I began to do a biblical study on the oil of God as it was used in the tabernacle and later in the temple in Jerusalem. It was a fascinating study, and I gleaned much revelation from the time I spent in the Word. I discovered two references to oil in Exodus 25:6, which is part of a list of items to be presented to God as an offering: *"[olive] oil for lighting, balsam for the anointing oil and for the fragrant incense."* From this verse, we can see that oil had a twofold purpose in God's house: it was used for light, and it was used for anointing.

God symbolically pours out His oil upon us through two distinct expressions:

1. God's oil brings light that causes us to shine with His radiance.
2. God's oil anoints us, consecrating us and setting us apart for His service.

Through Scripture, we understand that Jesus Christ—as the Messiah who fulfilled the law—manifests both of these realities for us as examples that we can follow. Let's examine in further detail how we see these expressions in Him.

"I AM THE LIGHT OF THE WORLD"

Long before Jesus walked on the earth, the Old Testament prophet Job spoke about a flow of oil filling his life like a river: *"My path was drenched with cream and the rock poured out for me streams of olive oil"* (Job 29:6 NIV). Today, we know that Jesus is the Rock (see 1 Corinthians 10:4), and it is through Him that we enter into the miracle streams of His oil.

God's oil flowed out through Jesus's life in such a plentiful way that He could announce, *"I am the Light of the world"* (John 8:12). Jesus has divinely instructed us to stay connected to Him so that we, too, can shine with His light.

> *You are the light of [Christ to] the world.... Let your light shine before men in such a way that they may see your good deeds and moral excellence, and [recognize and honor and] glorify your Father who is in heaven.* (Matthew 5:14, 16)

JESUS THE ANOINTED ONE

The Greek name *Christ* can be properly translated as "Anointed One." In Scripture, we see that Jesus was anointed by Father God:

> *God anointed Jesus of Nazareth with the Holy Spirit and with great power; and He went around doing good and healing all who were oppressed by the devil, because God was with Him.* (Acts 10:38)

Jesus was anointed to do good, to heal, to bring deliverance, and to set captives free. This special anointing from the Father flowed like the oil that was specifically reserved for His priests. You can receive this anointing too.

You may think, "Well, I'm not a priest!" According to Revelation 1:6, those who have committed their lives to Jesus Christ are indeed priests: He "*formed us* [those who have committed their lives to Him] *into a kingdom [as His subjects], priests to His God and Father.*" Through Jesus, we are the heaven-ordained ministers of God. And, through the Holy Spirit, we are being anointed to do the supernatural works of God.

AN ANOINTING EXCURSION

Recently, I was invited to speak at a conference in Boston, Massachusetts. This thrilled me because it had been nearly twenty years since I had ministered in that area of the United States. I felt a great expectancy about what God would do, but even my expectation couldn't compare to what happened over the course of the days I was there. In each meeting, the Spirit worked miracles and healings, and many people encountered God's manifest presence in a new way.

This gathering consisted of Pentecostal and mainline Protestants, Catholics, and Jewish believers. It thrilled me to see the unity of the Spirit being demonstrated among God's people. Our willingness to flow together with other believers will cause the oil of God to be poured out in greater measure.

After the second evening of meetings, I felt the Spirit compelling me and my team to physically anoint the region with oil. It was a big assignment, but I was delighted to receive this supernatural instruction. In obedience, we drove to one of the few stores open at that time of night and purchased every last bottle of oil from its shelves: peanut oil, vegetable oil, corn oil—any oil we could get our hands on. That night, we obtained fifty bottles in total, God's number of jubilee. Surprisingly, the store employees didn't bother to ask us why we needed so much oil; they simply provided us with several large boxes to carry the bottles in.

We were excited to be used in this mission of the Spirit, and we were eager to get started. Once we got back into the car, we turned on the "Atmosphere of Glory" soaking track that my wife, Janet, and I had recorded several years earlier along with a team of prophetic intercessors. This helped to set the atmosphere for what we were preparing to do. That audio track is composed of instrumental music complemented by prayers in heavenly tongues, and, as we listened to it, we joined in. We started praying in the Spirit and laying our hands on the bottles of oil we had just purchased, anointing them for God's purpose that night. When the Spirit directs you to lay your hands on certain objects as instruments for His glory, a powerful anointing is released to set them apart for His use. (See Exodus 40:9–11; Leviticus 8:10–11.)

That night, the Spirit directed us to drive to specific locations, and we anointed those places with the miracle oil for a twofold purpose, to God's glory:

1. To exercise our spiritual authority to supernaturally close and break agreement with any and all demonic agendas, assignments, or curses. The Bible says, "*It shall come to pass in that day that his burden will be taken away from your shoulder, and his yoke from your neck, and the yoke will be destroyed because of the anointing oil*" (Isaiah 10:27 NKJV). In the Spirit, the oil was marking a line that the enemy could not cross.
2. To prophesy into the atmosphere and decree a supernatural release of fresh anointing with the outpouring of the Holy Spirit. The Bible says, "*You will also declare a thing, and it will be established for you; so light will shine on your ways*" (Job 22:28 NKJV). Again, whatever we anoint, following God's divine instruction, will be set apart as holy. In the Spirit, the oil was marking a line to invite the presence of God to settle on particular places.

As the Spirit provided us with insight and navigated our journey, we could feel an increase and expansion of His anointing flowing and resting upon us and also upon the dark places to which we traveled. His light was shining ever more brightly as we poured the bottles of miracle oil in the specific locations He directed us to. We had complete confidence, knowing that God was at work and that, someway and somehow, we had a small part to play in the overall picture of what God would bring forth in fullness in the days to come.

MOVING AND FLOWING IN FAITH

Not long after our anointing journey, we received reports from the host ministry that God was blessing them with overabundant breakthrough. This included situating them in a new property and ministry building where they could expand their outreach. That was just the beginning of the miracles unfolding. They also reported an increase in angelic activity and a greater awareness of the glory realm, resulting in more healings and deliverances being observed in their ministry.

One evening, while I was ministering at Kingdom Awakening Ministries in Kingston, New Hampshire, the Spirit suddenly dropped a new song into my spirit, and I began to sing:

> There's an oily anointing in the presence of the Lord,
>
> There's an oil that's flowing in this place.
>
> It's an oil of healing,
>
> It's an oil of joy,
>
> It's an oil of breakthrough that's flowing in this place.

Once again, God was bringing us an obvious emphasis on His oil being poured out in greater measure. And it was bringing breakthrough to many people in attendance. Father Tom DiLorenzo, a charismatic Catholic priest from Boston, had come to the service with many other Catholic believers to receive a fresh impartation from the Spirit, and they certainly received it! Many of them were caught up in visions and encounters with the Lord as we sang the new song. I had originally hoped to spend some time talking with Father Tom at the end of the meeting, but he was caught up in a new anointing, and this anointing was increasing upon him. He couldn't speak, and I certainly didn't want to disturb the flow of the Spirit. When the anointing comes, we must submit our own desires to the Lord and learn how to yield to the Spirit's movement.

That night, some people asked me where they might purchase the new song I had sung, and I had to tell them it was a spontaneous song that had never been recorded before. It was the Spirit's *now* message to us.

Several weeks after I received this song, I was invited to speak to a church congregation in Birmingham, Alabama, about the feast of Hanukkah. This feast, which I describe in chapter 6, is all about the miracle of the oil. Following that meeting, several people commented to me that the message had been life-changing for them. One woman shared that she had taken the recorded message to a friend who was suffering from a life-threatening illness, and through the impartation of that message, the woman was completely healed. This was confirmed later that week by her doctor's reports.

Never be frightened to step out in faith and do your part, regardless of how small or how large that step may be. God needs each and every one of His children moving in faith and flowing with His anointing in this hour.

Let's pray together:

> Father, we stand in awe of You, Your power, and the miracles You work. We submit ourselves as candidates for a fresh touch of Your miracle oil so that we might be more effective lights in this dark world. Amen!

AS YOU CONTINUE TO READ THIS BOOK, IT IS MY PRAYER THAT YOU WILL CAPTURE THE ESSENCE OF GOD'S MIRACLE OIL IN YOUR SPIRIT, UNDERSTANDING THAT THERE IS MUCH DIVERSITY IN THE OUTPOURING OF GOD'S SPIRIT. MAY YOUR LIFE BE FILLED TO OVERFLOWING WITH *THE MIRACLE OF THE OIL*.

2

MIRACLE POWER

"You anoint my head with oil; my cup runs over."
—Psalm 23:5 (NKJV)

Have you ever tangibly felt the touch of the Holy Spirit flowing through your physical being? It is one of the most amazing and awesome things you can ever experience. It happens when the almighty God fills your spirit, your soul, and even your body with His presence to such a degree that it overflows from you.

As I previously mentioned, there have been several occasions when miracle oil has suddenly begun to flow from the palms of my hands, from the bottom of my feet, and even from my forehead. We should not be surprised when these things happen, because they can be one of the signs that God's presence is flowing in our lives.

THE OVERFLOWING PRESENCE OF GOD

Many years ago, I was ministering at a weekend conference in Coeur D'Alene, Idaho, along with several other ministers. As we gathered together, we could feel the precious oil of the Spirit coming to touch us in a personal way. Many people experienced manifestations of miracle oil. In each of the meetings, there was such a sense of God's presence in the oil. It manifested as a thick and beautiful fullness, with a distinct fragrance, a feeling of peace, and a spiritual weight that accompanies miracle anointing. My wife, Janet, has described it as having a cleansing effect on people, one that brings them an openness to God that enables them to respond to the way in which He is working.

One afternoon that weekend, as I was in my hotel room preparing for the meeting, prayerfully searching the Scriptures and seeking God for what He wanted to do, I suddenly began to feel oil physically forming in the palms of my hands. As is typical when oil supernaturally comes in this way, I first saw it appearing in the creases of my hands. Other people might disregard such a manifestation or write it off as sweaty palms or natural oils, but I've learned to discern the holy presence of God in it. Immediately, my heart turned to the Lord in worship. I thanked Him for what He was doing, and I invited the Spirit to increase the manifestation. I truly desire to be a vessel for the oil of God's presence, and I am always willing and eager for this miracle oil to flow in greater measure.

As I was seeking God in prayer and adoration, asking what He desired to do in the meeting that evening, the miracle oil increased. Soon it filled my palms completely and began to drip off them onto my wrists and fingers. The oil kept flowing, gently pouring onto my arms. I was being surrounded by a heavenly fragrance that smelled more extravagant than the most luxurious perfume. The scent was like that of dozens of roses filling the room with their elegant aroma. The aroma brought with it a sense of the beauty of God's holiness. This experience reminded me that Jesus Christ is called the Rose of Sharon, and He is the anointed Bridegroom who is soon returning for His church, the anointed bride. (See, for example, Revelation 19:7.)

On the bedroom dresser, there were two cups, which I used as containers to catch the oil. I rested each of my hands on the cups as the miracle oil gently flowed from my palms.

I continued to pray and seek the Lord, and His Spirit spoke directly to my heart, confirming with His gentle whisper the extraordinary sign of the miracle oil. I knew that my assignment that night was to speak about the power of God's anointing and His will that it flow—as the oil was now doing—like a river from the life of every believer who is completely committed to Christ and fully dedicated to the purposes of the Spirit.

As I pondered the message I was receiving, my hands continued to flow with this supernatural anointing oil until the oil began to spill over the tops of the cups. God was giving more oil than the vessels were able to hold. So, I set about to find another container over which I could rest my hands as the Spirit moved upon me in this unusual way. The only thing that seemed big enough was an ice bucket, so I retrieved it and rested my hands on its rim. For the next two and a half hours, the miracle oil maintained its flow.

Not only was the ice bucket filled, but I was also filled with an overflow of God's divine presence. The anointing was resting upon me in such a strong way that anyone entering the room could smell, feel, and spiritually sense the thick and oily presence of the Spirit.

"MY CUP RUNS OVER"

That day, in my heart, God reminded me of Psalm 23:5, where David sang,

> *You anoint my head with oil; my cup runs over.* (NKJV)

The revelation David had received was not about just a little bit of the miracle oil, not just a trickling, not just a tiny portion. His cup was overflowing, and so was mine. I knew that this was a message for me and also for the body of Christ as a whole. The Spirit desires to bring His anointed ones into the realm of overflow.

I believe that the supernatural flow of oil was and is a sign of God's superabundance, a sign of His overflowing goodness and His incomprehensible blessings. He desires to bring us all into such a place of overflow that we will no longer say, "I have nearly enough" or "I have just enough to begin doing what God has called me to do." He desires to fill us so full of His Spirit, so full of the golden oil from His throne, His heavenly enablement, the empowerment of the Holy Spirit, that it will overflow into and out of every area of our lives.

God desires to fill you so full that you will be overflowing in every way, that you will literally ooze with the miracle oil of His presence. It will pour out of who you are, and you will be able to stand with David and say, "God, You have anointed me with fresh oil to such a degree that it is overflowing. It is pouring forth from my life for Your glory."

> ***THE SPIRIT DESIRES TO BRING HIS ANOINTED ONES INTO THE REALM OF OVERFLOW.***

ANOINTED IN THE EVERYDAY

Believers have long recognized the need for anointed ministry. Anointed teaching is life-changing. In contrast, teaching that is not anointed puts us to sleep. What is being said may be good, but the way it is being served is boring and does not touch and move our spirits. The same, of course, can be said for preaching, testimony, music, and even prophecy. The touch of anointed miracle oil makes all the difference in the world.

Very often, however, we have not made this same important distinction about matters of business or private life. Believers often talk about a separation between what is sacred and what is secular, in an attempt to separate their spiritual lives from the necessary (and seemingly mundane) activities of their daily life. But God wants to so fill you with His Spirit that you can no longer separate who you are from who He is in you. In Him, you live and move and have your being. (See Acts 17:28.) Hallelujah!

We need anointed mail carriers, anointed doctors and nurses, anointed truck drivers, and anointed construction workers. We need anointed husbands, anointed wives, anointed mothers, and anointed fathers. This world would be such a better place if our schools were filled with anointed and caring teachers, if our government was filled with anointed public servants, and if our military was filled with anointed and dedicated soldiers. We all need the miracle of God's anointing oil, and we need it every day and in everything we do.

A LIFE-CHANGING ANOINTING

After hours of collecting the miracle oil flowing from my hands, I was convinced we were going to have an amazing anointing service that night. I knew the miracle of the oil served as a sign of the superabundant anointing that God was inviting all of us to experience in our own lives. As I ministered that evening, you could feel great expectation in the church sanctuary because the Spirit was performing signs and wonders, confirming the Word of God that was being preached. (See Mark 16:20.) As my message drew to a close, I invited those who were present to come forward to the altar, letting them know that I would lay my hands upon them and anoint them with the fresh oil God had provided.

I did not put just a little touch of oil on people's heads to anoint them that night. I used the oil liberally, sloshing it upon their heads so that it would drip down and cover them, symbolizing the superabundant anointing that was being released to them by the Spirit. It was powerful, wild, and exciting—and, for many people present in that meeting, it was indeed life-changing!

Recently, an Amish couple came to meetings I held in Chicago. They told me they had been present at the conference in Couer D'Alene years earlier, and they said, "You know, we've never been the same since that time. We're so passionate about Jesus that we just keep winning souls and healing the sick!" I was excited to hear that report! The anointing in their lives has lasted to this day.

During that time of ministry, I must have anointed hundreds of people with the supernatural oil, and yet there was more than enough oil for everyone. Some people who came forward received breakthroughs and deliverance from evil spirits that had been oppressing them. Others who came through the prayer line received marvelous healings and other physical miracles within their bodies. Some people even reported having out-of-this-world heavenly visions and encounters in the glory realm as they were anointed with the miracle oil. The manifestations of the Spirit's power that night were too numerous to count or record. There was an abundant outpouring of supernatural activity as we postured ourselves to receive the miracle power of God's anointing.

THE ANOINTED GOSPEL HEALS AND DELIVERS

Another time, when I was in Phoenix, Arizona, for ministry, miracle oil began to flow from both of my hands while I was worshipping the Lord in my hotel room before the meeting even began. I had been listening to Julie Meyer's album *Better than Life* and suddenly got caught up in the Spirit.

Ron Cocking, husband of Patricia King, came to my room to escort me to the service, but when he saw the flowing oil, he called the film team to come to the room to record this holy sign. Ron went into the bathroom and collected two cups for me to use to catch the oil. He brought them out into the living room where I was standing, and, as I placed my hands upon them, the oil continued to flow.

This manifestation was recorded as it was happening, and I'm so grateful for that because people from all over the world watched that recording on a DVD we put together at the time, and they were encouraged to receive an impartation from the Holy Spirit for themselves. As you can imagine, this recording of the miracle oil opened many doors for our ministry around the world. Such open doors are one of the results of the anointing.

Greater miracles were to come. When I went to the meeting, the oil kept flowing until it began dripping down onto the tops of my shoes. Prophetically speaking, one of the things our feet represent is the dispatch of the good news of the gospel. (See, for example, Romans 10:15; Ephesians 6:15.) Pools of the miracle oil began to collect, and then the oil started flowing *from* my feet. As I stepped out of my shoes and onto material that had been laid on the floor of the hall, the oil continued to flow, soaking the material with a tangible anointing of the Holy Spirit.

Later, while I was preaching, several ladies took that material upstairs and cut it into small squares to be used as anointed cloths to be distributed when we moved into the prayer-line ministry. We were following the pattern of the New Testament believers who distributed handkerchiefs and aprons that had touched Paul's body, and extraordinary miracles came forth.

> *God was doing extraordinary and unusual miracles by the hands of Paul, so that even handkerchiefs or face-towels or aprons that had touched his skin were brought to the sick, and their diseases left them and the evil spirits came out [of them].* (Acts 19:11–12)

During the ministry time, people received salvation, and many were healed of all manner of sickness and disease. One woman later wrote to our ministry, reporting that her womb had been miraculously opened. Doctors had said she could never conceive or carry a child, but one year later, she was holding her own baby girl in her arms! Another man testified to having been healed of stage 4 cancer, which never returned. Only God can do such miracles, and He often accomplishes them through the power of His anointing!

Let's pray together:

> Father, we need Your miracle power. We are nothing without You, but when Your power comes upon us and flows in us, we can do all things. Anoint us for miracle lives and miracle ministries. In Jesus's name, amen!

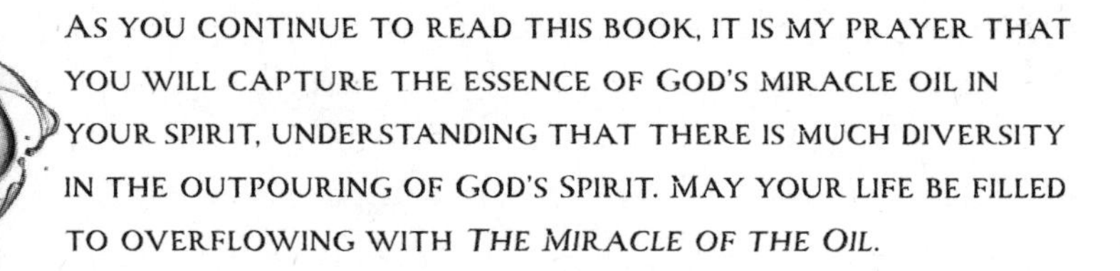

As you continue to read this book, it is my prayer that you will capture the essence of God's miracle oil in your spirit, understanding that there is much diversity in the outpouring of God's Spirit. May your life be filled to overflowing with *The Miracle of the Oil*.

3

MIRACLE PERCEPTION

"I kept looking in the night visions, and behold, on the clouds of heaven one like a Son of Man was coming."
—Daniel 7:13

I sensed a weighty presence of God's power. It was thick and electrifying, and I felt strong vibrations rippling throughout my physical body. This was a natural sign of something supernatural that was taking place. I had just arrived at the hotel where I was scheduled to minister at a Mountain Top Encounter minister's conference hosted by Dr. A.L. and Joyce Gill in Big Bear Lake, California, attended by ministers from all over the world.[1]

That evening, when I walked into the opening session, a cloud of glory was manifesting in the room. It was very thick, and I continued to sense spiritual tremors of God's power moving all over my

1. I also briefly wrote about this experience in my books *Moving in Glory Realms* (New Kensington, PA: Whitaker House, 2018) and *Seeing Angels* (New Kensington, PA: Whitaker House, 2019).

body. I could not put my finger on exactly what God was doing, but I knew that He *was* doing something. As we worshipped, the power of the Spirit continued to increase, so that my whole body trembled, as if waves of God's anointing were moving throughout me.

Later that night, when I was asleep, a bright and glorious cloud suddenly began to form before me. At first, it seemed to be just a white mist, swirling and filling the atmosphere in front of me. But then it grew until it became a cloud so large that I couldn't see the top or bottom of it. It was glorious, it was heavenly, it was unusual, it was extraordinary! I had been translated to a spiritual realm above the earth.

Then, from the front of the cloud, something like a swirling power portal opened, revealing a light. A huge holy angel appeared and moved toward me. His entire being seemed to shine, reflecting the light of God's radiant presence. This image was more wonderful than words could begin to describe. The angel was male in appearance, and yet he was so beautiful, reflecting the glorious atmosphere of heaven. He had long, flowing blond hair; porcelain skin; and strikingly brilliant blue eyes. Even his robes were dazzling and shimmering with the divine light. As I gazed at the angel, I knew that I was seeing a reflection of the glory of God. In that moment, all I could do was worship the Lord.

In his hands, the angel was holding an elegant golden bowl that was about five feet wide and six feet deep. As my eyes continued to behold the glory of God, the angel took the bowl and began tipping it toward where I was standing, pouring out its contents. Those contents streamed forth as golden oil, flowing down toward the earth below. The oil seemed limitless as it flowed out from the bowl.

Suddenly, I woke up. "It was just a dream," I thought, but it felt like so much more than that. And it was.

I glanced at the bedside clock. It was 2:35 a.m. Those numbers seemed familiar. I sat up and turned the lights on, knowing I wouldn't be able to sleep again after such an experience. Just then, I noticed that the atmosphere in the room had changed. Not only was the presence of the Lord filling the room, but sitting on the table at the end of my bed were two cups that had not been there when I went to sleep. Those cups were overflowing with an abundance of heavenly oil. Suddenly, it came to me:

> *You prepare a table before me in the presence of my enemies. You have anointed and refreshed my head with oil; my cup overflows.*

A prophetic scene of Psalm 23:5 was playing out before me.

DREAMS AND VISIONS

When miracle oil begins to flow in your life, it opens your spiritual eyes to see things that you've never seen before, as I did that night. This can happen during the day, and we would call that a vision. It can be perceptible as an open vision before you, or it can be an inner vision within your spirit. It can also happen at night, and we would call that a dream or a night vision. The difference between dreams and visions is that a dream has a symbolic interpretation, whereas a vision has a literal interpretation. God and His angels work through both of these realms. Peter spoke about dreams and visions in the prophetic word from the book of Joel that he released on the day of Pentecost:

> *"And it shall be in the last days," says God, "that I will pour out My Spirit upon all mankind.... And your young men shall see [divinely prompted] visions, and your old men shall dream [divinely prompted] dreams; even on My bond-servants, both men and women, I will in those days pour out My Spirit."*
>
> (Acts 2:17–18)

In many ways, God's oil is like an eye salve, an ointment placed upon our spiritual eyes that awakens them to see into the glory realms. When the miracle oil of God's Spirit is poured out upon us, our spiritual eyes are opened to behold His dreams and to see His visions.

We should expect greater vision, miracle vision, when the oil of God's Spirit is poured out in our lives because, again, this spiritual oil helps us to see what we have not seen before—including various tasks of God's angels. The Bible tells us that angels are ministering spirits sent to serve the heirs of salvation. (See Hebrews 1:14.) The Scriptures do not necessarily outline all of their ministry services. However, we do know that angels cooperate outwardly with the work of the Holy Spirit that is happening within us. In many ways, they are connected to the oil of the Spirit that flows in our lives.[2]

INCENSE AND GOLDEN OIL

Before I went to bed that night, I had placed my Bible on top of the entertainment cabinet in the hotel room. Yet it was now situated between the two overflowing cups on the table. And the pages of the Bible were covered in the visible shekinah glory of God, with golden particles sparkling across Revelation chapter 5.

I immediately picked up the Bible and began to read. The text spoke of the prayers of the saints going up like incense and being collected in the golden bowl. "*And when he* [the Lamb of God] *took the scroll, the four living beings and the twenty-four elders fell down before the Lamb. Each one had a harp, and they held gold bowls filled with incense, which are the prayers of God's people*" (Revelation 5:8 NLT). As I read, the Spirit began to speak to me about our praise and worship doing the same. In the meeting the night before, there had been a great shout of praise and a deep, intimate worship that had surely touched the throne of God.

Spiritually, I could see how our praise and worship would rise like incense to be collected in the heavenly bowl. Our anointed

2. For more specific teaching on the ministries of angels, please see my book *Angelic Activations* (New Kensington, PA: Whitaker House, 2021).

sounds were gathered in the bowl, and they became a golden oil that God desired to pour back onto the earth. This is the heavenly pattern that we see in the book of Revelation. The anointing was going up, and a greater anointing was flowing back down to us through God's manifest presence. As I worshipped the Lord in this atmosphere, I was beginning to capture this prophetic vision in my spirit. I stayed awake and began praying into the Word, reading the Spirit-highlighted chapter and asking God for increased revelation.

> ***OUR ANOINTED PRAISE AND WORSHIP ROSE LIKE INCENSE AND WAS COLLECTED IN THE HEAVENLY BOWL. IT BECAME A GOLDEN OIL THAT GOD DESIRED TO POUR BACK ONTO THE EARTH.***

SAP: SUPERNATURAL ANOINTING AND PROSPERITY

When I spoke at the meeting the next morning, the miracle oil began to flow once again. This time, it bubbled up in the palms of my hands and then ran down my wrists and fingers. It was literally dripping from my hands. Everyone who was present could see it.

At this point, I knew that God was divinely directing the meeting, so I stopped preaching and immediately instructed the people to line up around the outer walls of the conference room. The Spirit, I told them, was prompting me to lay my supernaturally anointed hands on each person who was willing to receive a fresh anointing.

The people present quickly followed my instructions, and we began to move into another level of God's power being released. I started at the front of the room and moved counterclockwise, anointing each person with the miracle oil that was flowing. The oil continued to manifest in my hands as I interceded for those who had come for prayer.

The oil that had overflowed onto my table at the hotel the night before had given off a unique fragrance. It had filled my room with the heavenly aroma of cedar, a supernatural scent that speaks of God's people overflowing with His goodness, power, and stability. Consider this Scripture:

> *The trees of the LORD are full of sap, the cedars of Lebanon which He planted.* (Psalm 104:16 NKJV)

Later, when I sought the Spirit for further understanding about this experience, He revealed to me by the Scriptures and my friend Joan Hunter, a healing evangelist, that when we operate in the anointing, as "the trees of the Lord," we are filled with spiritual sap. SAP is an acronym that stands for Supernatural Anointing and Prosperity.

As I ministered to the people at the meeting, the fragrance that had filled my room the night before was now emanating from my hands. It smelled wonderful! Prophetically speaking, it was like the sap from the cedars of Lebanon, flowing as an ever-increasing stream of anointing oil. It was dripping down my arms, falling from my hands, and pooling on the tops of my shoes—spilling out from the Holy Spirit within me and anointing those who had come and were ready to receive a powerful touch from the Lord.

One such person was a young girl who, unbeknownst to me, had been suffering from scoliosis. When I laid my oil-soaked hands on her head, instantly, her spine came into proper alignment. She was miraculously healed by the power of God!

Other miracles began happening all over the room—healings and deliverances. People were receiving miracles for their emotional needs as well as their physical needs. That day, I anointed all two hundred people in attendance. Then, once I had finished my time of ministry, the oil stopped flowing. It had come for a purpose, and that purpose had been accomplished. It was a glorious morning, with the Spirit of God orchestrating it all. Little did I realize that there was still something more that He would do!

A SUPERNATURAL OUTPOURING

Dr. A.L. Gill couldn't bring himself to close the meeting when it was time to do so. He sensed that there was still more that would be released for people to receive. And he was right.

Without warning, the keyboard that worship leader Steve Swanson had been using suddenly began playing by itself! A professional musician, Steve was very knowledgeable about this particular keyboard model, yet he was baffled about what was happening. There were sounds coming out of that keyboard that had not been programmed into its system. Steve threw his hands up in the air in amazement. Heaven had taken over his keyboard.

As the sounds came forth, it was clear that they were sounds from the heavenly realm. The anointing in the service that morning had unlocked a new realm of glory for us to explore. The Spirit of God allowed this unique manifestation to take place.

The keyboard continued playing on its own for about ten minutes. Then, again without warning, the atmosphere of glory suddenly shifted, and angels of God came down into the meeting. I didn't see them in that moment, and I don't think anyone else did either, but we could certainly hear them.

The voices of the angels were joining, in unison, with the heavenly sound from the keyboard. The angels began singing, "Holy, holy, holy!" Their voices rose until they could be heard above every other sound in the room. We could all hear them worshipping the Lord.

This angelic music was not coming through the sound system, and yet it could be heard all over the conference room. The room was literally filled with the angels' song. It surrounded us completely. The angels continued singing for another half hour, accompanied by the heavenly symphony coming from the keyboard.

As the angels sang, people fell on their faces before the Lord of glory. Some were weeping. Others were being filled with ecstatic joy. Many were lying prostrate in the Lord's manifest presence. It was a beautiful scene of supernatural outpouring. The anointing of God, through His miracle oil, had come to welcome His glory.[3]

A WORLDWIDE OUTPOURING OF GLORY

What the Spirit began in that Mountaintop Encounter didn't only remain on that mountain; it continued to flow through the lives of those who attended. From that day forward, we began to recognize a difference in the ease with which our ministry team functioned in the miraculous. Every place we went following that encounter, we saw an increase in angelic activity, an abundance of provision, and a wide array of extraordinary signs and wonders, with multiplied healings and miracles being reported. Soulwinning became easier, and deliverance occurred without exhaustive hours of ministry. My receiving the vision that night had been a defining moment for me and many others. Truly, what I had seen in that vision was now happening on earth.

In the following weeks, we ministered in Canada, South Korea, Japan, Florida, England, and France. In each place, we experienced an outpouring of glory, with great power being released! In addition, many of my ministry friends told me independently that, during this time, they felt a supernatural shift in the atmosphere in their own ministries. This glory movement seemed to be increasing all over the earth as God's people received a fresh anointing. What started as a divine vision was now becoming supernatural provision.

ANOINTED EYES

Will you receive a fresh anointing and vision today? Receive it for your life and for your ministry call. If you have felt stuck in

---

3. You might be wondering what happened to those two original cups that mysteriously appeared in my hotel room and that were filled to the brim and overflowing with the anointing oil. That oil was given to those who desired to carry it with them, to use as a miracle oil as the Spirit directed them.

your spiritual journey, just lift up your head to God and allow the Spirit to anoint your eyes. He wants to bring you a greater vision of His anointing. Just ask Him for it! Take time right now to ask the Lord to release His miracle oil upon your eyes so that you can better see Him and be aligned with His purposes. Lift your hands and say, "Lord, I receive this new anointing and vision."

> *Anoint your eyes with eye salve, that you may see.*
> (Revelation 3:18 NKJV)

Never discount what God shows you in the Spirit. A greater anointing is giving you access to a greater glory. But you must know it, and, spiritually speaking, you must see it, so that you can receive it! Keep in mind that you may not feel anything initially, but you can obtain it supernaturally in the Spirit by faith.

Let's pray together:

> Father, thank You for anointing our eyes with Your miracle eye salve and letting us see as never before the glories that await us in the realms of Your Spirit. Let us hear the sounds of the heavenly realm, and let us raise our voices in praise and worship that will ascend like incense to be collected in the heavenly bowl. Amen!

AS YOU CONTINUE TO READ THIS BOOK, IT IS MY PRAYER THAT YOU WILL CAPTURE THE ESSENCE OF GOD'S MIRACLE OIL IN YOUR SPIRIT, UNDERSTANDING THAT THERE IS MUCH DIVERSITY IN THE OUTPOURING OF GOD'S SPIRIT. MAY YOUR LIFE BE FILLED TO OVERFLOWING WITH *THE MIRACLE OF THE OIL*.

4

MIRACLE FAITH

"Jesus said, 'Let the children come to me. Don't stop them! For the Kingdom of Heaven belongs to those who are like these children.'"
—Matthew 19:14 (NLT)

When God anoints you for His purposes, He also anoints the pathway ahead of you. This includes providing you with divine connections and open doors of opportunity. I have discovered this truth time and time again in my own life and ministry. For example, many years ago, although I had never met him before, I received a phone call from Rev. Don Stewart, the successor to A. A. Allen's miracle ministry. Don called to ask me if I would come to his home in Scottsdale, Arizona, to spend the day with him and his family.

I was amazed by this divine connection. Early in our ministry, Janet and I had read Don's book *Only Believe*,[4] and it had provided us

4. Don Stewart, *Only Believe: An Eyewitness Account of the Great Healing Revival of the 20th Century* (Shippensburg, PA: Destiny Image Publishers, 1999).

with important insights and wisdom from the lives of God's "generals" whom He used in the healing revivals. Now, Don was calling me! Apparently, he had heard about how the Spirit had graced our ministry with extraordinary signs and wonders, and he wanted to speak into my life and also hear some of our miracle stories. The anointing on our lives had made a way for a divine connection. God's anointing is making a way for you, too, with divine connections and open doors!

CHILDLIKE FAITH RELEASES THE FLOW OF MIRACLE OIL

When the day came for me to visit Don at his home, we sat and talked for hours. Since that time, we have been great friends and have shared countless conversations. But I will never forget what Don told me that very first day: "Joshua, do you realize that the modern-day supernatural outpouring of miracle oil all started with a five-year-old boy? Childlike faith allows the anointing to flow...and that's why the anointing flows so easily for you." I was astounded because I didn't remember ever hearing this story before.

Excitedly, Don rushed me down the hallway toward his home office. There, he opened an old briefcase that contained several copies of *Miracle Magazine*, published by A. A. Allen. The atmosphere in Don's office was infused with expectation, and my heart was about to burst because I was eager to hear this testimony. For so long, I had felt all alone in ministry, facing persecution even from other believers and ministers who had misunderstood and misjudged me concerning the manifestation of miracle oil. I was delighted to find someone who had not only experienced this miracle firsthand but was also excited to talk about it and explain it a bit more!

Opening the pages of the November 1955 edition of *Miracle Magazine*, Don said, "I want to read you the story of Lavin Burcham, as told by his mother, Mrs. Sanders Burcham. This is the young boy who received the miracle oil." Here is a portion of what Don read to me:

> Lavin had hardly laid down in bed when he began to shout the praises of God and to speak in tongues. I knew that what was taking place was no commonplace experience. God was doing an unusual work.
>
> Then suddenly Lavin became very quiet. Big tears ran down his cheeks. Then suddenly he held out his hands. "Mother, Daddie! Look! Look at the oil Jesus is pouring on my hands!" he cried. "It isn't just plain oil. You can't buy this oil in the store. This is real oil, and it is coming from Jesus. Feel the oil, Mother and Daddie!"
>
> He placed his hands upon my cheek and upon his father's cheek. We could feel the oil on our faces.
>
> "Oh, Mother, Daddie, I can feel it all over me! Do you know what Jesus is telling me to do? He's telling me to take this oil and lay it on the sick and if they believe, they shall be healed."[5]

Don told me that upon hearing young Lavin's testimony and seeing the miracle oil appear on his hands, A. A. Allen invited Lavin to travel to several revivals with him. In Greensboro, North Carolina, as they were praying together for a dying man who was brought to the tent revival on a stretcher, the man immediately leaped up from his stretcher and walked away, totally healed by the power of God that was released as Lavin's hands touched him with the miracle oil. In a side article from the same *Miracle Magazine* issue, Mrs. Burcham was reported as saying that "when the anointing of the Lord is heavily upon little Lavin, his hands leave traces of oil on the foreheads of those whom he touches…although no oil is visible on his hands as he prays…."[6] This was another miracle of the oil, a real sign of the transference of anointing that was taking place in those moments.

I recently had the opportunity to speak with Rev. Lavin Burcham after the Spirit placed it on my heart to give him a call. Rev. Burcham

5. *Miracle Magazine: The Allen Revival News*, vol. 1, no. 2, November 1955, 10.
6. *Miracle Magazine*, 10.

and I had never spoken before, and I didn't have his phone number. But in a way that only God could do, the Lord provided me with Lavin's personal number, and when I called him, he told me he was celebrating his sixty-eighth anniversary in ministry! He felt that my call was a significant sign from the Lord on such a special occasion.

Ever since those days when he received the miracle oil as a young boy, Rev. Burcham has served the Lord faithfully. Between the ages of five and eight, accompanied by his mother, he traveled to twenty-eight states to minister. He has ministered as an evangelist in both the United States and Canada, preaching the gospel boldly to win lost souls and see the sick healed. He also pastored a church in North Carolina for almost thirty-five years.

The anointing comes to equip, empower, and enable us to do what God has called us to do. Receive a special anointing right now. It's available for you. Just sense the oily presence of God and His anointing filling you completely.

THE ANOINTING IS TRANSFERRABLE

In his book *Quantum Supernatural Power,* Don Stewart shared, "Sometimes hundreds of people in a single service would receive the supernatural outpouring of oil everywhere Rev. Allen put up the tent. Then it started happening in some churches. This was in the days before the internet, but it spread across America and around the world in a short period of time."[7]

Revivalist Ruth Ward Heflin also wrote about experiencing this wonderful corporate anointing for unusual signs and wonders:

> Before we were able to attend the meetings of Brother A. A. Allen for ourselves, we had heard people talking about the strange phenomenon being experienced in his meetings of oil appearing on people's hands and even

7. Don Stewart and Brendon Stewart, *Quantum Supernatural Power* (Tulsa: OK: Don Stewart Association, 2013), 198.

flowing from their hands. I was in my early teens by then and overheard preachers that I respected making fun of this phenomenon. They said, "It's nothing more than perspiration. They just rub their hands together and make them sweat. This is nothing more than a show. Everybody wants to get up front and be seen, and they will do anything to call attention to themselves."

Our parents never joined in these comments. They were wise enough to withhold judgment until they could see for themselves what was happening. They knew the Holy Spirit, and they were sure they would know the real from the false; so, until they had seen it for themselves, they would offer no opinion. I never heard either of my parents say anything critical about what someone else was experiencing in God. They were so hungry for God themselves that it made them open to new things. They didn't want to do anything that would hinder the move of God's Spirit.

We traveled from Richmond to Pittsburgh to be in the Allen meetings, and when we got to the tent, we found it to be packed with thousands of people. One of the first people who drew my attention was one of the ushers. He was leaning against a tent pole very near the back. His hands were behind him, resting on his hips, but he had his palms upward so that the oil that was coming from them would not drip onto his pants. He was not creating any sort of show. He was not waving his hands or showing them to anyone. He was just leaning against the pole, weeping and expressing his love to Jesus. When I saw this, my heart was totally melted. I realized that I had allowed the criticism I heard from others to get into my heart and affect my feelings about the oil on people's hands—even before I had personally witnessed it. Once I had seen it, I knew that it was of God.

> This man was one of thousands who experienced this in those meetings, and I believe we will see thousands again experiencing the same phenomenon.[8]

This anointing of miracle oil is transferable. Our ministry team has noticed that it increases the more that we speak about it, and that is one of the reasons I've written this book. I want you to receive an impartation as you read. We must be careful to honor and respect whatever the Spirit is doing. Keep your heart open to enter into His miracle flow. We have seen supernatural oil pouring forth in abundance to touch and minister to those who are willing to receive it.

MIRACULOUS HEALINGS

I was speaking at a summer camp meeting in Copetown, Ontario, Canada, when, about halfway through my message, as I was standing on the platform, the miracle oil began to flow from my hands and feet. A supernatural fragrance of rose flowers came from the manifestation on my hands. I proceeded to invite the host ministers, Pastors Russ and Mave Moyer, to smell my hands. As they did, Pastor Mave received an instantaneous healing in her knee, which had been out of joint and causing her great pain. She testified, "When I smelled the oil and went down [in the Spirit], I felt the heat run down my leg, and look at that [demonstrating lifting her knee]! There's no problem! You can feel it's right back in the right place! Hallelujah, thank You, Jesus!"[9]

In the same meeting, the fragrance of the oil covered the entire tent, and the majority of the people reported they were able to smell the heavenly scent. Because the oil was flowing profusely from my feet, I removed my shoes and proceeded to step on cloths

---

8. Ruth Ward Heflin, *Golden Glory: The New Wave of Signs and Wonders* (Hagerstown, MD: McDougal Publishing, 2000), 192–93. Used by permission of the Ruth Ward Heflin estate, Ashland, VA.
9. "Portals of Prosperity," Eagle Worldwide Retreat and Revival Centre, YouTube video, 27:25, September 5, 2009, https://www.youtube.com/watch?v=wXFZrCcpqgo.

and clothing items that were laid all over the altar area, anointing them with the oil so they could be used as a point of contact, such as I mentioned doing in an earlier chapter. (See Acts 19:11–12.)

Many miracles were reported from the anointing that flowed that night, including:

- People being healing of fibromyalgia, type 2 diabetes, and an irregular heartbeat
- An unsaved husband and his unsaved children making decisions for Christ after anointed cloths, soaked in the miracle oil, were placed under their bedsheets!
- A man unexpectedly receiving a pay raise after placing an oil-soaked piece of cloth in his wallet

As I have been describing in this book, God is releasing a great miracle anointing in the earth. All over the world, the Spirit is anointing His people for the miraculous. A woman in Brazil, whom I have met on several occasions, carries a very special touch of anointing upon her life that causes miracle oil to flow from her hands every day when she prays. Several years ago, we invited her to minister with us in Canada, and in those meetings, many unusual signs and wonders occurred. However, the greatest sign was the love of God that overflowed from her life as the miracle oil flowed.

One night, she prayed for every single person—hundreds of them. As was her custom, she gave them a hug and anointed them with this special oil. My friend Harold McDougal has written about this anointed woman, saying:

> She collects this oil in small sterile containers to use later to anoint those who have special needs. Because of her own miraculous healing from cancer, she has a particular burden for cancer patients, and many are healed of cancer when she prays for them and anoints them with this supernatural oil. I have personally been anointed with the

> oil on several occasions, and I can say that it has an aroma that I find unique. I have never smelled anything quite like it anywhere in the world.[10]

As we allow the miracle oil to flow, we also make room for the fragrance of heaven to fill our lives and the lives of those around us. God is giving us childlike faith to believe for the miracle of the oil to flow in our lives—both spiritually and physically—as we desire to receive it.

> *O LORD, our Lord, your majestic name fills the earth! Your glory is higher than the heavens. You have taught children and infants to tell of your strength....* (Psalm 8:1–2 NLT)

Let's pray together:

Father, thank You for sending Your anointing to those who have childlike faith in You, Your love, and Your miraculous power. Let us become like children in our faith so that the flow of Your oil will be released in our lives and continue to flow forth to be a blessing to others in our communities and around the world. In Jesus's name, amen.

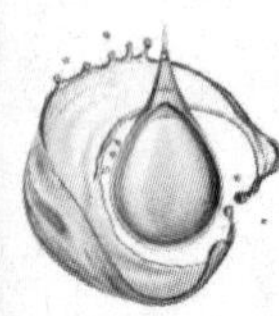

AS YOU CONTINUE TO READ THIS BOOK, IT IS MY PRAYER THAT YOU WILL CAPTURE THE ESSENCE OF GOD'S MIRACLE OIL IN YOUR SPIRIT, UNDERSTANDING THAT THERE IS MUCH DIVERSITY IN THE OUTPOURING OF GOD'S SPIRIT. MAY YOUR LIFE BE FILLED TO OVERFLOWING WITH *THE MIRACLE OF THE OIL*.

---

10. Harold McDougal, *Tokens of His Love* (Hagerstown, MD: McDougal Publishing, 2001), 26–27.

5

MIRACLE IMPARTATION

"The bottle of oil didn't become empty: GOD's promise fulfilled to the letter, exactly as Elijah had delivered it!"
—1 Kings 17:16 (MSG)

Overflowing supply, never-ending provision, abundance in every way...these are things we can expect as we tap into the miracle of the oil. For some, the idea of miracle oil may seem new. Yet, when we read through the Old Testament, we discover that God used supernatural oil to provide for His people even then.

Many people spend most of their Bible-reading time in the New Testament. Yet in the Old Testament, we find many stories that speak into our lives as Spirit-filled believers today. Much of what we read in the Old Testament is prophetic in nature—and we see its fulfillment overflowing in the New Testament, in church history, and even in our own lives. In the old covenant, we are given shadows, symbols, and types for what we can receive as believers under the new covenant, provided for us through the shed blood of Jesus Christ.

THE OVERCOMER'S OIL

In 1 Kings 17, we find a story of God's supernatural provision for a widow and her son. At the beginning of that chapter, we're told that a time of drought had fallen over the promised land. The Lord instructed His prophet Elijah to visit a widow who would provide him with food. Elijah arrived at the widow's house and requested, *"Please bring me a piece of bread"* (1 Kings 17:11). This was her reply:

> *As the Lord your God lives, I have no bread, only a handful of flour in the bowl and a little oil in the jar. See, I am gathering a few sticks so that I may go in and bake it for me and my son, that we may eat it [as our last meal] and die.*
>
> (1 Kings 17:12)

Elijah expected to be supplied with food and water. Instead, he found that the widow and her son were preparing to die of starvation! Elijah knew that the Lord had other plans for this woman. He instructed her to use her remaining food to bake *him* a loaf of bread—and then to bake another loaf for herself and her son. *"For this is what the Lord God of Israel says: 'The bowl of flour shall not be exhausted nor shall the jar of oil be empty until the day that the Lord sends rain [again] on the face of the earth'"* (1 Kings 17:14).

The widow, despite the drought, despite being on the brink of starvation, put her trust in the Lord and followed the instructions of His prophet, and the Lord indeed provided:

> *She and he and her household ate for many days. The bowl of flour was not exhausted nor did the jar of oil become empty.*
>
> (1 Kings 17:15–16)

"Nor did the jar of oil become empty." This widow experienced a bestowment of miracle oil! Whenever and wherever we honor the Spirit's anointing, we, too, should expect the miracle of the oil to flow with unlimited provision. Such provision includes:

- Heavenly guidance and wisdom to follow in God's ways
- An unusual and extraordinary flow of spiritual, emotional, and natural supply
- Divine covering for us and our loved ones

The anointing of the Spirit has been given to enable you to overcome in all situations and at all times, no matter how bleak your circumstances may appear. This is the overcomer's oil, the champion's oil. This is the miracle oil of breakthrough!

DIVINE INSTRUCTIONS PROVIDE DIVINE RESULTS

A few years ago, I was in my office when I felt the gentle whisper of the Spirit saying to me, "Joshua, I want you to find a bottle of pure olive oil and anoint it for My glory. Study the Scriptures about My anointing and then speak them over the oil. Allow Me to saturate you with My presence, and allow Me to infuse the oil with My miracle-working power. This oil must be set apart, for I will show you where and when it should be used."

After receiving these very clear instructions from the Lord, I set about to follow them exactly as the Spirit had spoken. I went to a local store and purchased a large bottle of pure olive oil. Then I brought it back to my office, and, with anointed worship music playing in the background, I began to type out a list of Scriptures I found pertaining to God's sacred anointing. In that moment, I could feel such a sense of heavenly glory in my office that it was almost overwhelming.

At one point, Janet came up to the office to speak to me, and she immediately asked, "What is happening in here?" She felt the same presence of God's glory that I did, and she wanted to be a part of it. Together, we took the Scriptures I had compiled and began to decree them over the bottle of oil. We knew that this was a divine assignment and that, as we followed the instructions of the Spirit, He would begin to work the miracles He had promised.

Once we had finished praying, we taped the list of Scriptures to the side of the bottle of oil. In this way, we were inviting the Lord to infuse this particular oil with His miracle-working Word. We set the bottle of oil on a shelf in my office and left it there, awaiting further direction from the Lord.

It must have been a couple of months later, while Janet and I were ministering at a summer camp meeting, that the Spirit spoke to me again about that oil, and the message was as clear as it had been before. "Joshua, tomorrow night, I want you to anoint everyone in this tent for an abundance of miracles."

I had heard God's voice, and now I knew what to do. There was only one problem: it was a two-hour drive from the camp meeting to our home, where the oil was sitting in my office. The next day, our schedule was full, so it was not possible for us to go home to retrieve the bottle. But God had spoken, so there had to be a way. When you know that you've heard the voice of the Spirit, you can have confidence that He will make a way for what He has spoken!

Janet soon discovered that Monique, one of our ministry board members, would be attending the camp meeting the following evening, so she gave Monique instructions for retrieving the bottle of anointing oil from my office, and she brought it with her. God had made a way!

The next night, an atmosphere of expectation filled the tent like a cloud of glory. Many people were ready to receive a fresh anointing, and when it came time for me to follow through with the Lord's instructions, I obeyed, anointing each person present for an abundance of miracles. This brought a miracle explosion! There were healings, deliverances, and a diverse array of signs and wonders. Pastors Russ and Mave Moyer, the meeting hosts, later commented on how thick the manifest presence of glory had been during that meeting.

However, something else remarkable happened that night. Although I had anointed hundreds of people, the level of oil in the bottle never dropped at all. That bottle was still full, similar to the experience of my friend Rev. Edgar Baillie with his bottle of supernatural oil, which I described in the introduction to this book. You might ask, "Joshua, maybe you used only a little bit of the oil?" On the contrary. I had used huge amounts of the oil when I prayed for the people that night. You could see the oil smeared across their foreheads as well as on their hands. When I anoint people with oil, I always do it the way the Bible describes people being anointed: I pour it on, smear it on, rub it on, and slosh it all around! But, miraculously, that night, after everyone had been prayed for, the bottle of oil remained absolutely full.

Although I had originally purchased that oil at a store, as directed by the Spirit, once Janet and I had laid hands on it and followed the divine directions given by the Lord, in some way, that natural oil had become infused with supernatural power. God wants to do a similar miracle for you. He wants you to offer Him what you have in the natural so that He can anoint it and use it supernaturally.

After the camp meeting, we continued to use that bottle of miracle oil as the Spirit directed. Sometimes we took it to the places where we ministered, and, at other times, we used it to respond to prayer requests we received through the mail. As the Spirit spoke to us to anoint a cloth for a specific need someone had written about, we mailed the anointed cloth to that individual. Still, no matter how much we used the oil, it never dissipated! To this day, I have that large container of anointing oil in our ministry office. It is filled to the brim and never runs out, no matter how much we use it as the Spirit directs us to. Following divine instructions provides divine results.

WHEN BAD THINGS HAPPEN TO GOOD PEOPLE

There is another story of a needy widow in the Old Testament that you might be familiar with. It is found in 2 Kings 4. The woman's husband, a prophet, had died, leaving her and their children in debt and in great need. In fact, if a solution could not be found, the children would be taken as slaves!

In those days, not just anyone could be called a prophet. It was an honored and revered position, and the prophets were limited in number. So we know that the woman's husband was a godly man who obeyed the Lord and walked closely with the Spirit. Even so, this man of God was suddenly taken from his wife and family, and they were left in a desperate position.

This type of situation is difficult to understand, isn't it? When bad things happen to good people, it can cause us to become confused regarding God's benevolence and loving-kindness. Some people struggle to understand how He could permit such devastation to occur in the lives of devout people. But stories like this widow's remind us of God's goodness and power to overcome even the direst circumstances. Sometimes we need to be reminded that when we struggle or grieve, God is still good. That's who He is. We don't hold all the answers, but He does. If we will give Him permission, He will take the most difficult situations and supernaturally turn them around, as we yield to the flow of His anointing.

Second Kings 4 tells us that the widow turned to the Lord's prophet Elisha for help. Elisha asked her what she had of value that she might sell. She replied, *"Your maidservant has nothing in the house except a [small] jar of [olive] oil"* (2 Kings 4:2). She didn't think it would be enough to save her, but Elisha knew otherwise.

> *He said, "Go, borrow containers from all your neighbors, empty containers—and not just a few. Then you shall go in and shut the door behind you and your sons, and pour out [the oil you have] into all these containers, and you shall set aside each one when it is full." So she left him and shut the door behind her and her sons; they were bringing her the containers as she poured [the oil]. When the containers were all full, she said to her son, "Bring me another container." And he said to*

> *her, "There is not a one left." Then the oil stopped [multiplying]. Then she came and told the man of God. He said, "Go, sell the oil and pay your debt, and you and your sons can live on the rest."* (2 Kings 4:3–7)

Can you see what happened here? This was another miracle of the oil. Just when it seemed that all hope was gone and there was nowhere to turn, God sent the overcomer's anointing to this widow's house through the prophet Elisha. The oil of provision showed up at just the right time, in just the right place.

We must remember that we live in a fallen world, one that is filled with darkness and troubles of every sort. This is a result of the original sin that occurred in the garden of Eden. Jesus Himself said,

> *"In the world you have tribulation and distress and suffering, but be courageous [be confident, be undaunted, be filled with joy]; I have overcome the world." [My conquest is accomplished, My victory abiding.]* (John 16:33)

Although there will continue to be afflictions in this world, as a believer, you can have bold confidence, knowing that you are an overcomer in Jesus. And, although problems may last for a night, the morning is coming, and, with it, the dawning of a new day. (See Psalm 30:5.)

You can trust that as you lean upon the Holy Spirit, He will turn things around for you, too, even in the most difficult of times. Press in to receive the fullness of God's anointing for your life, and do not give up. The miracle of the oil is available for you. When situations look dark, instead of faltering, stand fast in the Lord and believe for His miracle impartation for your need.

> ***PRESS IN TO RECEIVE THE FULLNESS OF GOD'S ANOINTING FOR YOUR LIFE, AND DO NOT GIVE UP. THE MIRACLE OF THE OIL IS AVAILABLE FOR YOU.***

ANOINTED MEN AND WOMEN IN THE BIBLE

At the conclusion to each chapter of this book, I have emphasized that there is much diversity in the outpouring of God's Spirit. When God pours out His miracle oil upon His people, it serves a specific purpose. We can see this clearly when we look at the lives of these biblical figures:

- Samson: the Breaker Anointing (See, for example, Judges 13:24–25; 15:14–15.)
- Saul and David: the Kingly Anointing (See 1 Samuel 10:1; 16:13.)
- David: the Music/Prophetic anointing (See, for example, 1 Samuel 16:14–23; 2 Samuel 23:1–2.)
- David: the Warrior Anointing (See Psalm 89:19–23; 2 Samuel 22:33–35.)
- Solomon: the Wisdom Anointing (See 1 Kings 3:5–12; 4:29–34.)
- Elijah: the Miracle Anointing (See, for example, 1 Kings 17:1, 14–16.)
- Elisha: the Double-Portion Anointing (See 2 Kings 2:9–15.)
- John the Baptist: the Prophetic Restoration Anointing (See, for example, Malachi 4:5–6.)
- Jesus: the Messianic Anointing (See, for example, Matthew 1:20–23; Philippians 2:5–11.) (Note: Jesus Christ, who was filled with the Spirit at all times, walked in the fullness of God's anointing and power. See, for example, Luke 4:16–20.)
- Peter: the Leadership/Teaching Anointing (See, for example, John 21:15–17; Acts 2:1–4; 14–41.)
- Stephen: the Servant's Anointing (See Acts 6:1–8.)

- Paul: the Apostolic Anointing (See, for example, 2 Corinthians 12:12.)

If anyone might think God's anointing is reserved only for men, I want to share with you a partial list of anointed women of God from the Bible. Throughout history, the Spirit has anointed both men *and* women for His purposes to be accomplished.

- Sarah: the Joy Anointing (See Genesis 21:6.)
- Miriam: the Prophetic Psalmist Anointing (See Exodus 15:20–21.)
- Deborah: the Mothering Anointing (See Judges 5:7.)
- Hannah: the Birthing Anointing (See 1 Samuel 1:15–20; 2:1.)
- Esther: the Favor Anointing (See Esther 2:17.)
- Priscilla: the Partnership Anointing (See Romans 16:3–4.)

Ask God to pour out His miracle anointing to fulfill His purposes in your life and in the lives of your loved ones!

Let's pray together:

> Father, I am in great need today, but I refuse to succumb to the mindset of an unbelieving world that says there is no hope. I depend on *Your* miracle impartation, and I know You will not fail me. Amen!

AS YOU CONTINUE TO READ THIS BOOK, IT IS MY PRAYER THAT YOU WILL CAPTURE THE ESSENCE OF GOD'S MIRACLE OIL IN YOUR SPIRIT, UNDERSTANDING THAT THERE IS MUCH DIVERSITY IN THE OUTPOURING OF GOD'S SPIRIT. MAY YOUR LIFE BE FILLED TO OVERFLOWING WITH *THE MIRACLE OF THE OIL*.

6

MIRACLE ILLUMINATION

"You shall command the Israelites to provide you with clear oil of beaten olives for the light, to make a lamp burn continually [every night]."
—Exodus 27:20

Several years ago, I recorded a holiday album called *Christmas Miracle*, producing the majority of it in Nashville and Hollywood. I had a wonderful time working on it, and it has become a blessing to many people around the world during the Advent season. As I was in the process of selecting which songs to include on the album, I came across a beautiful song entitled "Light One Candle" by Peter Yarrow of the folk group Peter, Paul, and Mary. It was a song about Hanukkah, and it resonated with me as a Spirit-filled believer because it deals with the importance of passing on the flame to change the world as we light those around us with the Light that has been given to us. I loved the imagery and symbolism of the menorah and candles, especially against the backdrop of the Christmas season. To me, that song paints a clear picture of what happens through the

Spirit's anointing. I've received many impartations through others who have been willing to share their light with me.

As a fifth-generation Pentecostal believer, I didn't grow up celebrating Jewish feasts like Hanukkah. That was just not something we Pentecostals did. We certainly loved Israel and prayed for the peace of Jerusalem, but we never paid much attention to any of the Jewish holy feasts. I guess, in some ways, we felt that the old covenant celebrations were for the past, and perhaps you feel the same way.

Yet, after hearing that Hanukkah song and beginning to do some research on the subject, I came to recognize that the Jewish feasts reveal to us the faithfulness of God, and there is so much joy, so much wonder, and so much glory that can be discovered through them. In the twenty-first century, we are privileged to see the heavenly pattern that began with Abraham, Isaac, and Jacob flowing into our present reality through salvation in the Messiah. There's a miracle oil that flows from the past, and if we will embrace this ancient anointing, it will open up new doors for our future.

As I mentioned earlier, to me, Hanukkah prophetically symbolizes the flame of the Holy Spirit being imparted from one person to another. In my life, it came about through the anointed impartation I received from my parents and grandparents and other charismatic elders who prayed over my life and passed to me the flaming baton. We have a responsibility to use the impartations given to us by the Lord in a way that honors Jesus and brings Him glory. We have the opportunity to do this every single day, everywhere we go.

A BACKGROUND OF DARKNESS

With this in mind, the celebration of the miracle of the oil at Hanukkah is certainly worthy of our consideration. The history of the commemoration of Hanukkah goes back to what are commonly called the "silent years." That's what theologians call the four hundred years between the pronouncements of the prophets Malachi and John the Baptist. During those years, not much seemed to be happening from a spiritual standpoint. It was the transition time between the Old Testament and the New Testament eras.

Although our Protestant Bibles contain very few details about the events that form the backdrop of Hanukkah, there are two books found in Catholic and Orthodox Bibles that deal with these events. Protestants consider these books to be part of the Apocrypha, which means "biblical or related writings not forming part of the accepted canon of Scripture."[11] To those who come from a Reformation heritage, these books have historical value, whether or not they are accepted as part of the Word of God. They help us to understand the customs and culture of biblical times.

There are two Apocryphal books in particular that deal with the subject of Hanukkah. They are 1 Maccabees and 2 Maccabees, and they explain in great detail the events surrounding the original Hanukkah celebration. As a lover of history and a researcher, I began to study these two books as well as other sources to learn more about this special feast. I found that the celebration has its roots in the second century before Christ and commemorates the restoration of Jewish worship in the holy temple in Jerusalem.

In the second century BC, Antiochus IV Epiphanes was reigning over the Jewish people. He was a member of the Seleucid dynasty, "a Greek dynasty ruling Syria and at various times other Asian territories from 312 BC to 64 BC."[12] His original name was Mithradates, but he later assumed the name Antiochus Epiphanes, which means "God Manifest." This tells us a lot about this evil king: he thought of himself as God and insisted that others do the same. It is not surprising that he was nicknamed Epimanes, meaning "Mad."

During Antiochus IV's reign, a lot of pressure was put on the Jews to forsake their cultural customs, their traditions, their worship of the one true God, and their desire to honor and obey Him in all

11. *Lexico*, s.v. "Apocrypha," https://www.lexico.com/en/definition/apocrypha.
12. *Merriam-Webster.com Dictionary*, s.v. "Seleucid," https://www.merriam-webster.com/dictionary/Seleucid.

things. They were being persecuted, and the temptation was to compromise, to "go with the flow." In 1 Maccabees 1:11, we read, "In those days certain renegades came out from Israel and misled many, saying, 'Let us go and make a covenant with the nations around us, for since we separated from them many disasters have come upon us.'"[13] These men had grown tired of resisting, tired of swimming against the current. It seemed to them that it would be so much easier to compromise. "If you can't beat them, join them." Isn't that what people say? Joyce Meyer has been quoted as saying, "Compromise means to go just a little bit below what you know is right. It's just a little bit, but it's the little foxes that spoil the vine."[14] This account certainly seems very relevant to the days we are living in right now.

The problem with this kind of thinking was that God had made a covenant with His chosen people, and they were forsaking that covenant. In 1 Maccabees 1:12–15, we read:

> This proposal pleased them, and some of the people eagerly went to the king, who authorized them to observe the ordinances of the nations. So they built a gymnasium in Jerusalem according to the customs of the nations, and made foreskins for themselves, and abandoned the holy covenant. They joined with the nations and sold themselves to do evil.[15]

One detail in this passage particularly caught my attention: "They...made foreskins for themselves." The phrase has also been translated as, "They...removed the marks of circumcision."[16] When I read this, I wondered, "Was that even possible? I know

13. *New Revised Standard Version, Updated Edition,* © 2021 National Council of Churches of Christ in the United States of America. Used by permission. All rights reserved worldwide.
14. "Joyce Meyer Quotes," Goodreads, https://www.goodreads.com/quotes/328238-compromise-means-to-go-just-a-little-bit-below-what.
15. *New Revised Standard Version, Updated Edition.*
16. See, for example, *Revised Standard Version of the Bible,* copyright © 1946, 1952, and 1971 the Division of Christian Education of the National Council of the Churches of Christ in the United States of America.

that all things are possible with God, but there are some things that seem impossible for man." I did some research and found that they had undergone a procedure known as *epispasm*, which is "a form of foreskin restoration to reverse circumcision, historically practiced among some Jews in Hellenistic and Roman societies."[17] Why is this important for us to understand? Because it shows the evil lengths to which people will go to defy God, to break covenant with Him and say, "I will no longer do what You have told me to do. I will now do things my own way."

I've found it notable that every Jewish feast is accompanied by readings from the Torah—except for Hanukkah. These Jewish feasts are not just parties. There is a spiritual reason for every celebration. The feasts came about for God-ordained purposes. Why, then, are there no readings for Hanukkah? It is generally accepted that 1 Maccabees was originally written in Hebrew. But that version has been lost, and only the Greek version from the Septuagint remains. Second Maccabees was written in Greek.[18] Greek would not have been spoken in the synagogues. However, it may also be because this incident is an embarrassing part of Jewish history. It depicts a time when there was a departure from the faith of the fathers. This was a very dark moment for the Jewish people.

In that time, the way society was going, for many people, it seemed easier to jump ship and start living like everyone else was. And so, one by one, the people who had been given to God and given to His covenant began making wrong choices. Their lifestyle was now blatantly opposing the ways of God. There was so much evil in that day, but is our day any different?

That was the chaotic climate that existed when Judas Maccabeus came on the scene. This man had a passion burning inside him, and that passion was so great that it sparked a revolt.

17. Word Finder, s.v. "epispasm," https://findwords.info/term/epispasm.
18. "The Books of the Maccabees," Britannica, https://www.britannica.com/topic/The-Books-of-the-Maccabees; "I and II Maccabees," Britannica, https://www.britannica.com/topic/biblical-literature/Greek-additions-to-Esther#ref597910.

He declared, essentially, "We must get back to what God told us to do. The covenant God made with us was real, and it was a blessing. What people are saying or doing cannot change that truth. God must have a people that will stand up for righteousness and holiness, a people that honor the covenant that has been given to them by the Spirit." Thankfully, many people listened to his impassioned pleas, and he led a revolt against pagan rule. Judas Maccabeus and the freedom fighters he inspired achieved victory against all odds.

A MIRACLE CELEBRATION

After winning the war, now known as the Maccabean Revolt, the Jewish people began to return to Jerusalem and to the temple. The soldiers who had fought for this victory were now employed in repairing the temple, preparing it for a return to holiness.

There was a lot to do. The pagans under Antiochus had violated the temple and stolen its most valuable treasures, including the sacred furniture. Missing were the golden altar, the golden lampstand, the sacred utensils, the table for the bread of God's presence, the cups for the drink offerings, the sacred bowls, the golden censors, the curtains, the crowns, and other golden decorations. The front of the temple had been stripped of silver and gold. In the place of the sacred items were statues of false gods. Judas Maccabees and his men were intent upon restoring this once-holy site for worship of the one true God.

When the work was finally finished, they decided to have a rededication ceremony. As part of that ceremony, they planned to light a menorah. However, a problem arose. They only had enough oil to last for a single day. The temple required a specific oil—a scarce, pure oil. It took a very careful process to prepare this oil, which I will describe in a later chapter. That very special oil was not available.

The passion in the heart of the Maccabees to rededicate the temple did not diminish, and they decided to light the menorah anyway and let it burn as long as it would. And that is where the miracle came in. By the supernatural intervention of God, the oil they had secured, enough for only one day, burned on for eight straight days. That miracle is what Hanukkah is all about. It celebrates the miraculous supply of oil and the miracle light it supplied.

THE LIGHT OF LIFE

Hanukkah is also known as "the Feast of Dedication," because it occurred while the temple in Jerusalem was being rededicated, or "the Festival of Lights," because of the miracle of light that took place in the temple. Interestingly, in the book of John, there is a record of Jesus celebrating this feast:

> *It was now winter, and Jesus was in Jerusalem at the time of Hanukkah, the Festival of Dedication. He was in the Temple, walking through the section known as Solomon's Colonnade. The people surrounded him and asked, "How long are you going to keep us in suspense? If you are the Messiah, tell us plainly."* (John 10:22–24 NLT)

It seems apparent that the question being asked of Jesus that day was only for the purpose of getting Him riled up. Instead, He riled up the demonic spirits influencing those who were tormenting Him by making this amazingly wonderful and seemingly outrageous declaration: *"I and the Father are One [in essence and nature]"* (John 10:30).

This statement was made at the time of Hanukkah, a celebration filled with symbolism. Jesus was saying to those fractious people, "I am right there in what you're doing, in what you're celebrating, in what you're talking about. That's Me, right there in the candle. I am the Light that never goes out." For the Jewish leaders, these were shocking statements, but a follower of Jesus can understand exactly what He was saying. Not long before this, He had stated,

> *I am the Light of the world. He who follows Me will not walk in the darkness, but will have the Light of life.* (John 8:12)

Jesus had declared Himself to be the Light, and this feast was all about miracle light. As everyone was concentrating on that miracle light, what better time to make Himself known? *"I and the Father are One,"* He said. He was the Light that came to give people *"the Light of life."*

THE FESTIVAL OF LIGHT TODAY

In the days of Judas Maccabaeus, God saw the hearts of those who were passionate for Him, and He provided the oil for the lamp supernaturally. This resulted in a season of great rejoicing among the people. And, because of the amazing event that happened in Jerusalem so many years ago, Jewish people all over the world celebrate Hanukkah to this day. During the days of Hanukkah, the menorah, with all its symbolism, is lit every evening at dusk.[19]

What does Hanukkah mean for Spirit-filled believers in the twenty-first century? The candle in the middle of the Hanukkah menorah is called the servant (or helper) candle. With our spiritual eyes open, we can see that this candle represents Jesus Christ. Each night during the feast of Hanukkah, the servant candle is lit, and it is then used to light the other candles. As Christians, we, too, receive our light from Jesus.

The first night of Hanukkah, only the servant candle and the candle to the far right are lit. The second night, the servant candle is lit and then it is used to light the next new candle, the second from the right, and then the one to the far right again. In this way, each evening, a new candle is lit, moving from right to left, as well as the other candles that have previously been lit, moving from left to right, until, on the final night, all nine candles are lit.

Each time the servant candle is used to light a new candle or the previously lit candles, it is returned to its place. It is always the central candle, and all the other candles receive their light from it.

---

19. There are nine candles in the current menorah used by celebrants, rather than seven, as in the original menorah that was lit daily in the temple.

This is the beautiful symbolism of Hanukkah, and it is a revelation of Jesus and His central place in our lives. Without Him, all is darkness. With Him, we walk in glorious light.

EMBRACING THE ANCIENT ANOINTING

The festivals and feasts practiced in the Old Testament and instituted during the intertestamental period may seem like relics of the past. Yet God's calendar has never changed, and He still honors the set times that He appointed as days to recognize important spiritual transitions moving into the promises of God. (See Leviticus 23:2.) As new covenant followers of Christ, we are welcomed by the Spirit to join in the celebration of these feasts through our love for Jesus and God's chosen people, the Jews. This is a special invitation that we receive today, and we should respond by opening our hearts to learn and gain deep insight from all that the Spirit desires to reveal.

> ***THERE IS AN ABUNDANT SUPPLY OF MIRACLE OIL AVAILABLE TO YOU SO THAT YOU MIGHT SHINE FORTH IN THIS DARK WORLD AND LIGHT OTHERS AROUND YOU.***

The more I've come into deeper revelations of the anointing, the more, it seems, I have connected with the very heart of God. The things that are on God's heart are now on mine, as well, as I joyfully join in celebrating the feasts of the Lord. For instance, I have received a deeper desire to pray for Israel, to bless God's people, and to seek the truth about God's dealings with His people down through the ages.

The festival of Hanukkah, especially, is a celebration of renewed hope. The light that shone in that temple in the second century before Christ was miraculous and brought glory to the one true and living God, and He is still the Father of Lights:

> *Every good thing given and every perfect gift is from above; it comes down from the Father of lights [the Creator and Sustainer of the heavens], in whom there is no variation [no rising or setting] or shadow cast by His turning [for He is perfect and never changes].* (James 1:17)

You and I must remember that Jesus is the true Light of the world and that our God is a God of abundant miracles. His miracle oil is still flowing to us today. There is a superabundant supply of miracle oil available to you so that you might shine forth in this dark world and light others around you.

Let's pray together:

> Heavenly Father, Your Spirit brings the miracle of illumination to our lives. You are glorious, and Your words and works are beyond compare. Thank You that You bring us into divine revelation. Thank You for the powerful anointing of Your Holy Spirit. Thank You for placing Your anointing oil within us. In this way, You bring us into Your light and allow Your light to shine through our lives. In these dark days in which we live, help us to radiate the light of Your Spirit to the world around us so that people might see and know You! May we increase in Your miracle anointing more and more, for the glory of Your name and the building of Your kingdom. In Jesus's mighty name, amen!

AS YOU CONTINUE TO READ THIS BOOK, IT IS MY PRAYER THAT YOU WILL CAPTURE THE ESSENCE OF GOD'S MIRACLE OIL IN YOUR SPIRIT, UNDERSTANDING THAT THERE IS MUCH DIVERSITY IN THE OUTPOURING OF GOD'S SPIRIT. MAY YOUR LIFE BE FILLED TO OVERFLOWING WITH *THE MIRACLE OF THE OIL.*

7

MIRACLE RECIPE

"Take for yourself the best spices...."
—Exodus 30:23

In the Scriptures, we read how God's people, following His instructions, prepared special oils for sacred uses. In Exodus 30, God spoke to Moses in the wilderness about the makeup of the sacred oil for use in the portable tabernacle, the place where God's presence rested above the ark of the covenant. The Lord said:

> *Take for yourself the best spices: five hundred shekels of liquid myrrh, half as much—two hundred and fifty—of sweet-scented cinnamon, and two hundred and fifty of fragrant cane, and five hundred shekels of cinnamon blossom according to the sanctuary shekel, and a hin of olive oil. You shall make of these a holy anointing oil, a perfume mixture, the work of a perfumer; it shall be a sacred anointing oil.* (Exodus 30:23–25)

Here we can see that the anointing of God must be highly valued. The passage goes on to provide instructions for using this oil to anoint only specific objects and people, like the high priest. (See verses 26–33.) Today, when operating in the anointing, we need to closely follow the leading and guidance of the Holy Spirit.

This is such an amazing passage of Scripture! God was revealing to His people the sacred recipe for the anointing oil to be used for holy purposes. The Spirit was giving the Israelites understanding through what we might today call "a supernatural download." He was revealing His secrets. This was a divine recipe, the exact ingredients in their exact measurements required to create the special anointing oil. How remarkable!

There is so much glory in the Word! The Word is living and breathing (see Hebrews 4:12), and it comes alive for us as we posture ourselves to receive God's revelation. In the Bible, you can read about something as arcane (to most people) as lineage and be blessed and transformed. If you have ears to hear, eyes to see, and a spirit to recognize what God is saying, the blessing is there for you in every part of His Word. There are revelations awaiting your discovery. That is no less true concerning the makeup of the sacred anointing oil.

When God gave these ingredients, He was introducing us to the depths of His Spirit. He was telling us the full function, the full ability, the full unction that is available to us in the anointing. That is the importance of the miracle of the oil!

In the next few chapters, we will take these ingredients one by one and explore their meaning for us today. First, let's consider a few important implications of the above passage and the recipe it delivers.

OBEYING DIVINE INSTRUCTIONS

As we previously discussed, over and over again in the Scriptures, we see that obedience to God always positions us to receive what He desires to release to us. Why did He give the anointing oil recipe to Moses? It was so that Moses could properly anoint the priests, ordaining them for service in the work of the ministry, enabling them to be prepared and equipped.

The real miracle recipe in the life of any believer is simply to follow whatever instructions God provides. Beyond the specific commands of Scripture that apply to everyone, that might look like one thing for certain people, and something completely different for others. But the important thing is to listen carefully and to obey what we hear. Deuteronomy 28 is a classic passage on this subject. First, God showed the Israelites what they would receive through obedience, and then He showed them what they would lose through disobedience. His message began:

> *Now it shall be, if you diligently listen to and obey the voice of the LORD your God, being careful to do all of His commandments which I am commanding you today, the LORD your God will set you high above all the nations of the earth. All these blessings will come upon you and overtake you if you pay attention to the voice of the LORD your God.*
>
> (Deuteronomy 28:1–2)

Although this is an Old Testament admonition, it lays down a timeless spiritual principle: as we follow God's lead, we are lifted up and positioned to do great things for Him. Obedience is the place of miracles, the place where we are raised above sickness, poverty, and despair. This doesn't mean that we won't face those "giants"; it simply means that we don't need to be afraid of them. We can have peace and confidence because God is giving us supernatural instructions that will lead us into the manifestation of His promises. When we follow the Spirit's leading and live in obedience to the vision God gives us, we will receive a heavenly recipe for success, in every sense of the word.

THE REAL MIRACLE RECIPE IN THE LIFE OF ANY BELIEVER IS SIMPLY TO FOLLOW WHATEVER INSTRUCTIONS GOD PROVIDES.

Another verse from the Old Testament that talks about the blessings that come from following God's instructions is Deuteronomy 5:33:

> *You shall walk [that is, live each and every day] in all the ways which the* Lord *your God has commanded you, so that you may live and so that it may be well with you, and that you may live long in the land which you will possess.*

The miracle of divine provision becomes ours as we listen to and obey the recipe that God gives us for our lives. A major part of that recipe is to follow what God's Word says to do. The Bible is filled with divine instructions and perfect guidance for living. However, another aspect to that recipe is the voice of the Spirit, who speaks to us, as followers of Christ, even today. Both facets must be a daily part of the Christian's way of life. A good New Testament teaching about this principle is found in James 1:22:

> *But prove yourselves doers of the word [actively and continually obeying God's precepts], and not merely listeners [who hear the word but fail to internalize its meaning], deluding yourselves [by unsound reasoning contrary to the truth].*

It is not enough to *receive* the recipe; we must *do* the recipe. It is not enough just to have it in our minds, or even to write it out and hold it in our hands. In order for the recipe to take effect, we must move into action, putting its instructions into practice.

Jesus taught us the importance of aligning our lives with His character and purposes. He expressed how our obedience creates a habitation for God's miracle power to rest on and within us:

> *If anyone [really] loves Me, he will keep My word (teaching); and My Father will love him, and We will come to him and make Our dwelling place with him.* (John 14:23)

Again, a recipe can be a wonderful thing, but we must follow it in order to reap the expected benefits.

> ***IT IS NOT ENOUGH TO RECEIVE THE RECIPE. IN ORDER FOR THE RECIPE TO TAKE EFFECT, WE MUST MOVE INTO ACTION, PUTTING ITS INSTRUCTIONS INTO PRACTICE.***

NO LIMITS IN GOD

As I expressed earlier, if God gave Moses such wonderful and detailed instructions for producing the sacred anointing oil with which to anoint the priests, then He will also speak to you today, as a priest unto Him, and give you a recipe to equip you for success in life. He can show you what to eat or not eat, or what to do or not do to improve your physical health. He can show you how to improve your marriage, or how to be a better mother or father, wife or husband, daughter or son. He can give you the key to healing a broken relationship. God can give you a detailed plan for a successful business venture. He can inspire you to design new inventions.

There are no limitations when you are willing to hear and obey the voice of the Spirit. Ask the Lord to begin to reveal His full recipe for your life today!

Let's pray together:

> Father God, here I am. Show me Your spiritual recipe for success in my life's endeavors, as I remain guided by You. Help me to respond to You and Your instructions, obeying You fully. For Your glory, amen!

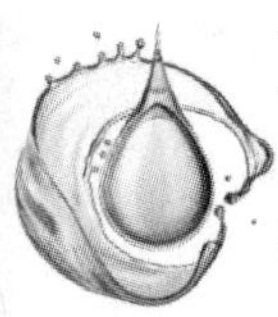

AS YOU CONTINUE TO READ THIS BOOK, IT IS MY PRAYER THAT YOU WILL CAPTURE THE ESSENCE OF GOD'S MIRACLE OIL IN YOUR SPIRIT, UNDERSTANDING THAT THERE IS MUCH DIVERSITY IN THE OUTPOURING OF GOD'S SPIRIT. MAY YOUR LIFE BE FILLED TO OVERFLOWING WITH *THE MIRACLE OF THE OIL*.

8

MIRACLE FLOW: LIQUID MYRRH

"Take for yourself the best spices: five hundred shekels of liquid myrrh."
—Exodus 30:23

The first ingredient God gave Moses for the sacred anointing oil was the spice *"myrrh."* The Israelites were to use five hundred shekels of it, which is equivalent to about two hundred ounces or twelve and a half pounds. That was a lot of myrrh. What did using so much myrrh indicate? It signified that it was to be a superabundant anointing.

All myrrh is precious, but the Israelites were to use a very particular type: liquid myrrh. To me, this ingredient represents a free-flowing anointing, an anointing without hindrance.

WHAT IS MYRRH?

Myrrh was one of the gifts the wise men presented to Jesus after His birth because it was among the most valuable substances on earth. Part of what gives it its value is the difficult process of making it. The normal process involves first slicing the bark of a thorny tree. This allows the liquid inside, the sap, to drip out. As the drops of myrrh sap gather over time, the liquid begins to solidify into a gummy substance, a resin. This resin can then be collected.

However, the instructions God gave to Moses specifically stated that the myrrh for the anointing oil had to be liquid, or free-flowing. Since the myrrh came out slowly in drops, this meant someone had to watch the process and be ready to catch enough of the precious element to meet God's requirements. Can you imagine how many thorny trees would have been needed and how difficult it would have been to gather that substance when it was still a liquid? No wonder it was so costly!

BITTER AND BROKEN

When we think about God's anointing, we like to focus on His power, healing, breakthroughs, and all the other wonderful things that come as a result of the miracle oil of the Spirit. Yet the inclusion of myrrh as one of the critical components of the anointing oil reminds us that sometimes we must first go through a process in which God prepares us to receive His anointing.

> ***IF YOU ARE WILLING TO RELEASE THE BITTERNESS IN YOUR LIFE TO GOD, HE WILL INCREASE THE ANOINTING AND POUR OUT MORE OF HIS OIL IN AND THROUGH YOU.***

Consider again the production of myrrh. In order to obtain this substance, producers must slice the bark of the tree. This process brings to mind suffering, affliction, and brokenness—subjects most of us try to avoid. Yet the truth is that in order to fully receive what God has for us, we have to be willing to allow Him to make "incisions" in our lives where we need to change and grow; and, many times, this is a painful process. Yes, it can hurt, but when you get past all your "stuff" and get into the Spirit, receiving His healing and strength, you will not be sorry!

Another aspect of myrrh is that it is extremely bitter. I got a little on my lips one day when I was experimenting with it, and I could still taste it hours later. The bitterness of myrrh represents the bitter things we sometimes have to go through in life. The Spirit is faithful to carry us all the way through our difficulties as we offer this bitterness to God. If you are willing to release the bitterness in your life to Him, He will increase the anointing and pour out more of His oil of gladness in and through you. (See Hebrews 1:9.)

DEATH TO SELF AND SANCTIFICATION

There is a reference to myrrh in the story of Jesus's birth, but we also find a reference to it in relation to His crucifixion and death. In the gospel of John, we read the following:

> *With him* [Joseph of Arimathea] *came Nicodemus, the man who had come to Jesus at night. He brought about seventy-five pounds of perfumed ointment made from myrrh and aloes. Following Jewish burial custom, they wrapped Jesus' body with the spices in long sheets of linen cloth.*
>
> (John 19:39–40 NLT)

In biblical times, myrrh was used in the burial process. In this passage, Joseph and Nicodemus used approximately seventy-five pounds of mixed oils—including myrrh—to prepare Jesus's body for burial. Myrrh is associated with death. For Christians, this aspect of the anointing oil particularly represents a sacrificial death to self, like that which Paul wrote about in Galatians 2:20:

> *I have been crucified with Christ [that is, in Him I have shared His crucifixion]; it is no longer I who live, but Christ lives in me. The life I now live in the body I live by faith [by adhering to, relying on, and completely trusting] in the Son of God, who loved me and gave Himself up for me.*

The ingredient of myrrh reminds us that God increases His anointing when we truly come to the end of ourselves and lay our lives—with all our desires, hopes, and dreams—at the foot of the cross. "*Those who belong to Christ Jesus,*" according to Galatians 5:24, "*have crucified the sinful nature together with its passions and appetites.*" The anointing helps to change our focus from being *self-conscious* to being *God-conscious.*

As I indicated in the previous chapter, we learn from Scripture that the anointing oil was used for sanctifying items in the tabernacle, as well as for consecrating the high priest for his sacred duties. That was one of the instructions God gave Moses: "*You shall anoint Aaron and his sons, and consecrate them, that they may serve as priests to Me*" (Exodus 30:30 NKJV). In Leviticus, we read how Moses obeyed this command.

> *And he poured of the anointing oil upon Aaron's head, and anointed him, to sanctify him.* (Leviticus 8:12 KJVER)

Several dictionary definitions of *sanctification* include "the action of making or declaring something holy," "the action or process of being freed from sin or purified," and "causing something to be or seem morally right or acceptable."[20] God's anointing leads us

---

20. *Lexico,* s.v. "sanctification," https://www.lexico.com/en/definition/sanctification.

to die to self while enabling us to live from the Spirit. When the anointing begins to work in our lives, it helps us to put the fleshly nature to death so that we might live through the freedom of the Spirit. This process can feel very challenging if we are still trying to live according to the flesh. But a person who is dead doesn't feel anything. So, let the Holy Spirit do His work in you. Yield to the process, submitting to God's work of sanctification.

A BEAUTIFUL SURRENDER

Think back to the events of the first Hanukkah, particularly the miraculous provision of oil. Remember that the miracle oil began to flow when the people repented of their own ways, got fed up with the pagan ways of the world, and rededicated themselves to God. It flowed when they decided to serve Him in the only right way—God's way.

Jesus spoke of our need to surrender to Him and to be willing to "endure whatever may come" for His sake:

> *If anyone wishes to follow Me [as My disciple], he must deny himself [set aside selfish interests], and take up his cross daily [expressing a willingness to endure whatever may come] and follow Me [believing in Me, conforming to My example in living and, if need be, suffering or perhaps dying because of faith in Me].* (Luke 9:23)

We must make a decision to let go of whatever has tried to hold us back from pursuing God and follow Him in total obedience. Nothing less will do.

When we consider the wonder of God's love, joy, peace, and all the other goodness that is available for us in Him, what could possibly hold us back from full surrender? What could be worth failing to embrace and receive all that He has for us. Let it go!

Think of specific areas in your life that you feel the Spirit is asking you to lay down in burial. Add them to the holy anointing oil of the recipe for success God is giving you. Give these hindrances to Him in sacrificial surrender.

As you let go of whatever has been holding you back from pursuing God in total obedience, yield yourself to Him, as the golden candlestick of the Lord, and decree with me, "Spirit, flow through me! Spirit, be my supply! Spirit, lead and guide me. I surrender all to You, and I do it now."

NOTHING TO FEAR

Feel the love of God that is flowing to you right now. There is nothing to fear about surrender when you know that His love is present with you. His love dispels all fear, and you are released from all fear through His perfect love. (See 1 John 4:18.) Fear can no longer be part of your life. In its place, divine love guides you.

When we prepare God's recipe His way, miracles happen!

Let's pray together:

> Thank You, Jesus, for the myrrh. Thank You for brokenness and surrender. Thank You for burial. Your body was broken for me, and I choose to open myself to Your will. Help me to become free of anything that would hinder the miracle flow of oil in my life. Jesus, I lay it all down at Your feet. My greatest desire is to glorify You. Amen!

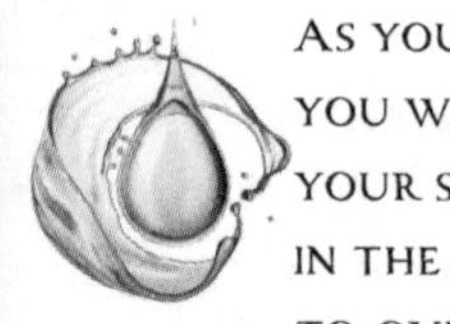

AS YOU CONTINUE TO READ THIS BOOK, IT IS MY PRAYER THAT YOU WILL CAPTURE THE ESSENCE OF GOD'S MIRACLE OIL IN YOUR SPIRIT, UNDERSTANDING THAT THERE IS MUCH DIVERSITY IN THE OUTPOURING OF GOD'S SPIRIT. MAY YOUR LIFE BE FILLED TO OVERFLOWING WITH *THE MIRACLE OF THE OIL.*

9

MIRACLE PRAYER: SWEET CINNAMON

"Take for yourself the best spices:...half as much—two hundred and fifty—of sweet-scented cinnamon."
—Exodus 30:23

The second ingredient of the holy anointing oil was *"sweet-scented cinnamon."* Many of us don't have firsthand experience with myrrh, but most of us are very familiar with cinnamon. It may be among the spices in your own kitchen. The Israelites were to use two hundred and fifty shekels of cinnamon, which is equal to about one hundred ounces, or a little over six pounds. What do we add to myrrh, which represents self-denial and suffering? We add what follows such surrender and sacrifice: sweet intimacy with God.

SWEET INTIMACY WITH GOD

The following imagery from Song of Solomon, which includes a mention of cinnamon, speaks of the marriage chamber, the place of intimacy:

> *Your shoots are an orchard of pomegranates, [a paradise] with precious fruits, henna with fragrant plants, fragrant plants and saffron, calamus and cinnamon, with all trees of frankincense, myrrh and aloes, along with all the finest spices.*
> (Song of Solomon 4:13–14)

When we live a life of intimacy with the Lord, we receive His revelation. In a state of intimacy, nothing is hidden. Everything is open and exposed. The ingredient of cinnamon is therefore a call for transparency. God calls us into a loving relationship with Him so that He can share His secrets with us, and, in turn, we can allow ourselves to become unashamedly open before Him.

In intimacy, the oil of the Spirit begins to flow. We receive God's miracle oil as we spend time with Him, being honest and vulnerable, and as we worship Him in the way He so richly deserves. This kind of intimacy is sweet.

WHEN WE BECOME THE WORSHIP, WE BECOME THE INCENSE; WE BECOME THE SWEET-SCENTED CINNAMON, EMANATING THE AROMA OF INTIMACY.

The concept of "*sweet-scented*" cinnamon is connected to worship. Our worship is like incense that ascends to the throne of God. We must position ourselves in such a way that we not only give God worship, but our lives *become* worship unto Him. When we become the worship, we become the incense; we become the sweet-scented cinnamon, emanating the aroma of intimacy.

When we come into the Lord's presence as worship unto Him, the miracle oil begins to flow. The oil is certain to be poured out in greater measure when we open ourselves up to God in this beautiful way.

THE ANOINTING IS FATNESS

As an incense, cinnamon also prophetically represents intercession or prayer for breakthrough. The Scriptures declare,

> *The yoke will be destroyed because of the anointing oil.*
> (Isaiah 10:27 NKJV)

What does that statement mean? Other translations use "*fat*" in place of "*anointing oil.*" Both translations are correct, but we find a deeper meaning in the word "*fat.*" This is not considered a positive word in our current cultural climate because fat is generally something we all try to avoid. However, in a spiritual sense, fatness speaks of supernatural expansion, taking new territory, the anointing increasing until the chains break. And this can only happen through intercession.

You may find that as you are engaging in your normal prayer duties, suddenly, through the anointing, the Spirit will take you into new places in prayer, and you will find that your spiritual reach begins to broaden into a breakthrough for you and for others.

SWEETNESS COVERING US

Cinnamon, like myrrh, comes from the bark of a tree. We typically use cinnamon when it is finely ground into a powder. However, if you examine a cinnamon stick, you can see that the ground version starts out as bark. Bark is a covering. Therefore, cinnamon also represents spiritual mantles and spiritual coverings. We give God our old mantles, the difficult things we have carried, and He provides us with His blessing of new coverings through the anointing.

When we come to the heart of God, we discover that His sweetness covers us:

> *To grant to those who mourn in Zion the following: to give them a turban instead of dust [on their heads, a sign of mourning], the oil of joy instead of mourning, the garment [expressive] of praise instead of a disheartened spirit. So they will be called the trees of righteousness [strong and magnificent, distinguished for integrity, justice, and right standing with God], the planting of the* Lord, *that He may be glorified.*
>
> (Isaiah 61:3)

THE WORD OF GOD

Not only is cinnamon prophetic with regard to worship and spiritual coverings, but the Hebrew word for cinnamon, *qinnamon* (using English letters), comes "from an unused root (meaning to erect); cinnamon bark (as in upright rolls)."[21] In the cinnamon stick, can you see an image of a scroll or the Torah?

The Torah represents the Word of God. The reason God's Word must come forth in the anointing oil is that the Word and the Spirit work together to cause divine growth. The Word brings truth, and the Spirit brings power. Jesus is the living Word of Life, and when the anointing of the Spirit is flowing with Jesus, miracles happen!

Let's pray together:

> Lord, I thank You for the sweet scent that is being released through our prayers and worship. It is causing a greater anointing to come upon us, an anointing that we are releasing to others. It is an anointing that breaks chains. Thank You, God, that the chain-breaking anointing is

---

21. *Strong's Exhaustive Concordance of the Bible*, #H7076, electronic version, © 1980, 1986, and assigned to World Bible Publishers, Inc. Used by permission. All rights reserved.

a component of the sacred oil. Through the oil of Your Spirit, captives are being set free. Children and grandchildren who were lost are coming home. Father, I thank You that families are being restored because of the anointing that destroys the yoke of the enemy. I offer my lips for Your anointing to flow. *"Let the words of my mouth and the meditation of my heart be acceptable in Your sight, O Lord, my Strength and my Redeemer."*[22] In Jesus's name, amen!

AS YOU CONTINUE TO READ THIS BOOK, IT IS MY PRAYER THAT YOU WILL CAPTURE THE ESSENCE OF GOD'S MIRACLE OIL IN YOUR SPIRIT, UNDERSTANDING THAT THERE IS MUCH DIVERSITY IN THE OUTPOURING OF GOD'S SPIRIT. MAY YOUR LIFE BE FILLED TO OVERFLOWING WITH *THE MIRACLE OF THE OIL*.

---

22. Psalm 19:14 (KJVER).

10

MIRACLE HEALING: FRAGRANT CANE

"Take for yourself the best spices:
...two hundred and fifty of fragrant cane."
—Exodus 30:23

The third ingredient of the miracle anointing oil used in the wilderness tabernacle was "*fragrant cane.*" Some Bible translations use the word *calamus* instead of fragrant cane. Just like cinnamon, the measure of this ingredient was a little over six pounds.

Fragrant cane is a plant that likes to grow near water. Historically, the root has been used medicinally. It is still used in some medicines and as an essential oil and healing aid today. Through the elements of the sacred anointing oil, God is revealing to us secrets of the Spirit, the wonderful spiritual benefits of His anointing—which include healing. *"But for you who revere my name, the sun of righteousness will rise with healing in its rays"* (Malachi 4:2 NIV).

OIL AND HEALING

Scripture makes many connections between oil and healing. In Old Testament days, the priests, after confirming that a leper was healed, followed God's instructions for the full cleansing of the healed person. Such cleansing included the application of both oil and blood from sacrifices. (See Leviticus 14:10–18.) The use of blood and oil is symbolic to us today of the blood of Jesus coming together with the power of the Spirit's anointing to bring about the full manifestation of divine healing:

> *Is any sick among you? let him call for the elders of the church; and let them pray over him, anointing him with oil in the name of the Lord. And the prayer of faith shall save the sick, and the Lord shall raise him up; and if he have committed sins, they shall be forgiven him.* (James 5:14–15 KJV, KJVER)

In Mark 6:13, we read how Jesus's twelve disciples *"cast out many demons, and anointed with oil many that were sick, and healed them"* (NKJV). In the parable of the good Samaritan, the Samaritan used oil and wine (spiritually representing healing and salvation) to minister to the wounds of the weary traveler who had been robbed and beaten:

> *And went to him, and bound up his wounds, pouring in oil and wine, and set him on his own beast, and brought him to an inn, and took care of him.* (Luke 10:34 KJV)

> ***THE OIL IS NOT A MAGICAL FORMULA OR SPECIAL POTION DESIGNED TO CURE THE SICK. JESUS CHRIST IS THE HEALER—AND HE IS THE ONLY HEALER.***

There is so much spiritual symbolism in the use of anointing oil when praying for people's healing. However, we must realize that, although there may be healing properties within the oil, in itself, the oil is not the healer. It is not a magical formula or special potion designed to cure the sick. Jesus Christ is the Healer—and He is the only Healer. We must look to Him at all times and never lose sight of this miracle-working truth.

OIL IN HEALING MINISTRY

When we choose (or are specifically instructed by the Spirit) to use oil in the process of ministering healing to those who are diseased, ill, or lame—as we see indicated in the Scriptures—the anointing must be accompanied by intentional, faith-filled, commanding prayer. This is indicated in the passage from James 5 above. Such faith is the key to activating the healing power of God's anointing. You must speak in faith while applying the oil, which, again, is symbolic of the Holy Spirit's power. In this way, you activate the power of God and give the recipient a point of contact to receive their divine miracle.

Look at some of the instructions in the Word of God concerning ministering healing in this way:

- ***"Let them pray over him"*** **(James 5:14 KJV, KJVER).** The Greek word translated as *"pray"* in this Scripture is *proseúxomai,* which means "to pray—literally, to interact with the Lord by switching human wishes (ideas) for His wishes as He imparts faith ('divine persuasion')."[23]
- ***"The word is near you; it is in your mouth"*** **(Romans 10:8 NIV).** When you receive inspired faith for someone's healing, a declaration of your faith must be spoken into the atmosphere. You must be willing to speak what you know by the Spirit. Your God-given decree activates a flow of healing miracle oil in the life of the receiver.

23. "HELPS Word-studies, #G4336, proseuchomai," Bible Hub, https://biblehub.com/greek/4336.htm.

- ***"Whatever things you ask for in prayer [in accordance with God's will], believe [with confident trust] that you have received them, and they will be given to you"*** **(Mark 11:24).** To offer true prayer is to be willing to speak boldly, asking God for His promises to manifest, knowing that it is His will to accomplish and demonstrate His Word on the earth.

We need to ask for and receive the flow of God's miracle oil for healing on behalf of ourselves and others. If you are in need of healing, right now, place your hands on your head and receive the flow of healing oil from the Spirit, praying the following prayer in faith.

Let's pray together:

> Lord, You forgive all my iniquities. You heal all my diseases. You redeem my life from destruction. You crown me with loving-kindness and tender mercies. You satisfy my mouth with good things, so that my youth is restored like the eagle's.[24] Father, I pray in faith, believing that I am healed. I am whole. I am holy. I am filled with Your light, Your love, and Your glory. Thank You, Lord, for Your healing anointing, Your healing power, Your healing touch! Hallelujah! In Jesus's name, amen!

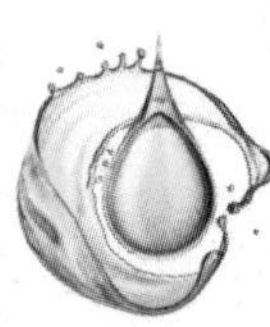

AS YOU CONTINUE TO READ THIS BOOK, IT IS MY PRAYER THAT YOU WILL CAPTURE THE ESSENCE OF GOD'S MIRACLE OIL IN YOUR SPIRIT, UNDERSTANDING THAT THERE IS MUCH DIVERSITY IN THE OUTPOURING OF GOD'S SPIRIT. MAY YOUR LIFE BE FILLED TO OVERFLOWING WITH *THE MIRACLE OF THE OIL.*

---

24. See Psalm 103:3–5.

11

MIRACLE UNITY: CASSIA

"Take for yourself the best spices:
...five hundred shekels of cinnamon blossom [cassia]
according to the sanctuary shekel."
—Exodus 30:23–24

The fourth ingredient of the anointing oil for the wilderness tabernacle was cassia. Cassia is sometimes confused with cinnamon. However, although the two ingredients are related, they are distinct. The instructions in the recipe for the anointing oil say to use five shekels of cassia, which is the equivalent of about two hundred ounces, or over twelve pounds. Cassia is used as a warming spice, and it represents hospitality.

HOSPITALITY AND UNITY

This fourth ingredient of the anointing oil increases in our lives as we become hospitable to the presence of the Holy Spirit and as we become more hospitable toward others. The dictionary defines hospitality as "the friendly and generous reception and entertainment of guests, visitors, or strangers."[25]

One of the specific purposes of the anointing is to draw believers together. When we extend hospitality to others in God's name, we open ourselves up to a unity with them that only the Lord can produce. Consider these words from Psalm 133, which are sometimes referred to as "the Commanded Blessing":

> *Behold, how good and how pleasant it is for brothers to dwell together in unity! It is like the precious oil [of consecration] poured on the head, coming down on the beard, even the beard of Aaron, coming down upon the edge of his [priestly] robes [consecrating the whole body]. It is like the dew of [Mount] Hermon coming down on the hills of Zion; for there the LORD has commanded the blessing: life forevermore.*
>
> (Psalm 133:1–3)

How good it is for brothers and sisters, the people of God, to come together or dwell together in unity! The psalmist compared such unity to the precious oil of consecration poured on Aaron's head, which ran down over his beard and onto his priestly robes, consecrating his whole body. He also likened unity to the dew from Mount Hermon coming down on the hills of Zion, covering them completely. *"For there,"* he said, *"the LORD has commanded the blessing: life forevermore."* We can think of it this way: through the power of the Spirit, the anointing starts at the Head, Jesus Christ (the Anointed One), and covers the entire body of Christ.

I love that imagery. Our willingness to lay down our differences with others, to set aside the things that have separated us, is pleasing to God and results in divine blessing for us. Being hospitable brings with it automatic blessing. How good and how pleasant is that! This is a recipe for divine goodness.

---

25. *Lexico*, s.v. "hospitality," https://www.lexico.com/en/definition/hospitality.

COMMON GROUND WITHOUT COMPLACENCY

Although, in the natural, we may not have much common ground with some members of the body of Christ, in the spiritual realm, all the members of Christ's body are united through the anointing of the Spirit. *"And it is God who establishes us with you in Christ, and has anointed us"* (2 Corinthians 1:21 ESV). Stepping into the hospitable nature to which God calls us requires us to focus on our unity in the Spirit.

I want to emphasize that finding common ground with our brothers and sisters in the Lord does not mean that we become complacent or lukewarm. It does not mean that we no longer stand for our personal convictions of what is right. It means that we make a conscious decision to come together in the Spirit, to come together around the person of Jesus, our common Savior. We are united not because we agree on everything but because we all belong to Him. This means that we are no longer self-focused. We are now God-focused. We have gotten to the point where we take our eyes off what is earthly and temporal, and focus on what is heavenly and eternal.

For example, we stop focusing on the color of someone's skin. We stop thinking about who is right and who is wrong in a particular conflict. We choose not to be offended by the way someone talks or the way they make us feel. Instead, we look to the Lord and say, "God, I want to be in unity with You, and that means I must be in unity with Your whole family. I choose to come together with all Your children in the unity of the Spirit." The anointing helps to guard our hearts against offense—being offended by God or by other people.

STEPPING INTO THE HOSPITABLE NATURE TO WHICH GOD CALLS US REQUIRES US TO FOCUS ON OUR COMMON GROUND IN THE SPIRIT.

THRIVING IN UNITY

Thus, the ingredient of cassia encourages divine connection for supernatural growth. God is not expecting you to just survive—He wants you to thrive! And you can thrive when you are anointed by God's miracle oil and planted among other Spirit-minded individuals. Thank God for the warm hospitality that comes into your heart from the Spirit of God to embrace the things of God and the people of God.

Let's pray together:

> Lord, I thank You that You are introducing us to new ways and new days, to new opportunities and new divine connections. We yield ourselves to Your miracle unity. Help us to love as Jesus loved, which includes loving the unlovable and forgiving others as we have been forgiven, for the sake of Your kingdom, honor, and glory. Amen!

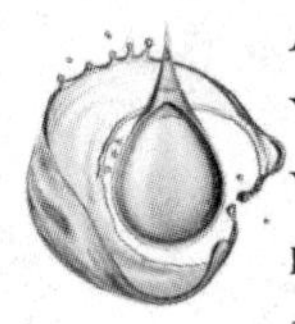

As you continue to read this book, it is my prayer that you will capture the essence of God's miracle oil in your spirit, understanding that there is much diversity in the outpouring of God's Spirit. May your life be filled to overflowing with *The Miracle of the Oil*.

12

MIRACLE PURITY: OLIVE OIL

"Take for yourself the best spices:...a hin of olive oil."
—Exodus 30:23–24

Thus far, we have considered four of the five specific ingredients that compose the holy anointing oil. It is significant that the oil has five ingredients in total. Five is the number of grace. If you want the miracle anointing to increase in your life, you must accept the free gift of God's grace through Jesus Christ, for He is the Anointed One. In addition, you must receive the infilling of the Holy Spirit, which is also given to us by grace.[26]

The fifth and final ingredient was *"a hin,"* or about one and a half gallons, *"of olive oil."* With this final ingredient, the anointing

26. In my book *Power Portals* (New Kensington, PA: Whitaker House, 2020), I teach on how to receive the infilling of the Holy Spirit. Please see chapter 2, "Finding Your Way," pages 58–60.

oil was complete. The olive oil we use today is a common enough ingredient. However, the oil called for in this recipe was not just any olive oil. It required the purest oil.

"VIGOROUS YOUNG OLIVE TREES"

Before we talk further about the oil itself, let's look at its source, the olive tree. Recently, while preparing for her ladies' Bible study, my mother felt led to look into deeper meanings of the olive tree. Examining Psalm 128, she was intrigued by verse 3, which says, in part, *"Your children will be like vigorous young olive trees as they sit around your table"* (NLT).

When we grow and mature before the Lord with pure hearts, like healthy young olive trees, we will bear much fruit. The anointing comes with God's grace for fruitful abundance. In my own experience, the more I increase in the anointing, the greater results I produce. Through God's anointing, we become fruitful in soulwinning, in ministering healing to the sick, and in casting out evil spirits. So much fruitfulness!

> *When you produce much fruit, you are my true disciples. This brings great glory to my Father.... You didn't choose me. I chose you. I appointed you to go and produce lasting fruit, so that the Father will give you whatever you ask for, using my name.* (John 15:8, 16 NLT)

PEACE AND PURITY

The very first time we find a biblical reference to the olive tree, it is in relation to the dove that brought an olive leaf to Noah while he and his family were still in the ark after the flood. (See Genesis 8:11.) That symbolic gesture spoke of peace between God and man.

Our peace with God is based on our right standing before Him in Jesus Christ. God looks for those who are pure; and what God receives, He also purifies.

> *Dear friends, now we are children of God, and what we will be has not yet been made known. But we know that when Christ appears, we shall be like him, for we shall see him as he is. All who have this hope in him purify themselves, just as he is pure.* (1 John 3:2–3 NIV)

The anointing is a call to holiness, drawing us to pour out our repentance before the Lord but also to receive complete forgiveness of our sins in Christ. A divine exchange occurs in which our sin, which Jesus paid for, is removed from us, and we receive Jesus's righteousness and holiness. "*If we confess our sins, he is faithful and just and will forgive us our sins and purify us from all unrighteousness*" (1 John 1:9 NIV).

Through the anointing, God's miracle oil sets us apart and consecrates us as pure and holy to the Lord. In this way, we feel the grace and godly weight of responsibility to operate in God's call, given to us by the Spirit, which causes us to walk softly and humbly before Him.

The genuine anointing of the Spirit does not "puff us up" or make us proud. It brings us into a place of greater surrender to the Lord. In the anointing, we learn the importance of yielding to the flow of God so that we can say, as Jesus did, "*Not My will, but Yours, be done*" (Luke 22:42 NKJV). This leads to ongoing peace with God and purity of heart.

BEATEN, NOT CRUSHED

Recall that, at the first Hanukkah celebration, the Hebrew people did not have available the oil that they needed. Why? Because the type of oil required for the temple was a very pure oil that resulted from a specific production method. And just as pure oil was required for the tabernacle and temple worship, it is pure oil that God is releasing into our lives through the anointing of His Spirit.

In ancient times, there were two methods for producing olive oil. The first method involved crushing the olives. When you crush olives, you retain the outer skin, the meat, and everything else. This method produced a lesser-quality oil that the people of Israel used for lighting oil lamps, for cooking, and for other household uses. However, as I mentioned previously, this type of oil would not do for holy service to God in the temple.

The finer oil used for the lamp in the tabernacle as well as in the anointing oil recipe required a second method of production. This method, mentioned in Exodus 27:20, involved beating the olives:

> *You shall command the Israelites to provide you with clear oil of beaten olives for the light, to make a lamp burn continually [every night].*

According to *Strong's Concordance,* the Hebrew word translated *"beaten"* comes from the root word *kātat,* among whose meanings is "to break in pieces."[27] When you break an olive into pieces, it releases the pure oil from within.

Try it some time. Break open an olive and remove the pit. Notice the few drops of precious oil that are released? That is the pure oil to which the Bible is referring. It's like a bit of liquid gold.

It is a lot easier to take the complete olive and grind or press it to extract the oil. When you do that, much more oil can be harvested. Again, this type of oil could be found in abundance in and around Jerusalem. The pure oil, however, was special and rare.

---

27. *Strong's Exhaustive Concordance of the Bible,* #H3807, electronic version, © 1980, 1986, and assigned to World Bible Publishers, Inc. Used by permission. All rights reserved.

A MIRACLE FLOWING

When we understand these two types of olive oil and how they are produced, we can comprehend the miracle of Hanukkah a bit more fully. It wasn't that there was no olive oil in the entire region. No, the pagans were having a heyday; they had a lot of oil, and they used it for many different things. But it wasn't the holy oil. It wasn't the costly oil, the most valuable oil. It wasn't oil that required time and effort and sacrifice. For the menorah, the very best oil was necessary.

Why do you suppose God caused the light to shine for eight days? And what do you suppose the Jewish people were doing during all that time? You can be sure they were not off partying somewhere or just wasting their time. They all knew that a miracle was in progress, and the more days that passed, the greater the miracle became. This caused awe and wonder among the people. And it gave them more time to get together the required oil, more time to gather the firstfruits of the available olives. It is said that it would take them seven days to collect enough olives, break them open, and extract the precious firstfruits oil in order to light the menorah for another week. God was giving them special favor.

This was the miracle of the oil. It flowed with power, and it kept on flowing for eight days. Whenever God's people pursue Him, despite their difficult circumstances, they can be assured of this promise:

> *And we know [with great confidence] that God [who is deeply concerned about us] causes all things to work together [as a plan] for good for those who love God, to those who are called according to His plan and purpose.* (Romans 8:28)

Miracle oil flowed for Judas Maccabeus and his freedom fighters in the second century before Christ, and miracle oil is flowing for you today. Lift your hands to the heavens and receive it. The miracle of the oil is for your life and the lives of those you love—*and it is yours today.*

Let's pray together:

> Father, You call us to purity. We want more of You manifesting in our lives. We ask You to perform in us the miracle of purity by Your Spirit as we respond to your call to holiness. I thank You for the supernatural oil You are releasing to Your people today. Thank You for divine revelation that comes to move us from where we have been into the place You have prepared for us. Continue to unfold to us Your plan, step by step, little by little, as we go from faith to faith, from strength to strength, and from glory to glory.
>
> Lord, I thank You that the miracle of the oil is an ever-increasing miracle. Right now, Lord, You are causing a greater anointing to be established within us. We receive it, and we rejoice in it. As Your anointing oil flows through us, there is nothing too difficult for us to accomplish. Nothing is too hard for You, and, because we believe in You, and You live in us, nothing is too hard for us either. Nothing is impossible when the miracle of the oil is flowing to us. We believe, and we receive. In Your mighty name, amen!

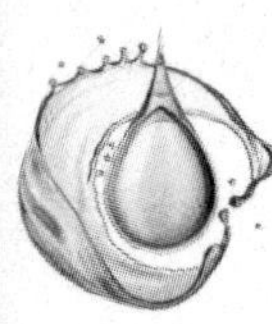

AS YOU CONTINUE TO READ THIS BOOK, IT IS MY PRAYER THAT YOU WILL CAPTURE THE ESSENCE OF GOD'S MIRACLE OIL IN YOUR SPIRIT, UNDERSTANDING THAT THERE IS MUCH DIVERSITY IN THE OUTPOURING OF GOD'S SPIRIT. MAY YOUR LIFE BE FILLED TO OVERFLOWING WITH *THE MIRACLE OF THE OIL.*

13

MIRACLE ANOINTING

"The Spirit of the Lord God is upon Me, because the Lord has anointed Me."
—Isaiah 61:1 (NKJV)

God wants our lives to overflow with His miracle oil! Being a Spirit-filled believer means that you have had an initial experience of being filled with the Holy Spirit, and you also choose to live the Spirit-filled life. It means you continually walk in the power of the anointing.

We gain great insight into God's anointing and the responsibility that comes with it when we read these words from the prophet Isaiah, a portion of which we looked at earlier:

> *The Spirit of the Lord God is upon Me, because the Lord has anointed Me to preach good tidings to the poor; He has sent Me to heal the brokenhearted, to proclaim liberty to the captives, and the opening of the prison to those who are bound; to proclaim the acceptable year of the Lord, and the day of vengeance of our God; to comfort all who mourn, to console those*

> *who mourn in Zion, to give them beauty for ashes, the oil of joy for mourning, the garment of praise for the spirit of heaviness; that they may be called trees of righteousness, the planting of the* Lord*, that He may be glorified.* (Isaiah 61:1–3 NKJV)

This passage shows us that God's anointing does not come just so that we can get goosebumps, experience the electricity of the Spirit, feel a warmth in our bodies, or sense the tingling vibrations of the spirit realm. That is not the purpose of the anointing. Those may be some of the manifestations of the anointing, but the purpose of the anointing is that we may do the works of God on the earth. It's the anointing that activates the gifts of the Spirit into operation. (See, for example, Romans 12:6–8; 1 Corinthians 12:7–10; Ephesians 4:11; 1 Peter 4:10–11.) God desires to perform supernatural works through natural vessels like us.

> ***THE PURPOSE OF THE ANOINTING IS THAT WE MAY DO THE WORKS OF GOD ON THE EARTH, SUPERNATURAL WORKS PERFORMED THROUGH NATURAL VESSELS.***

A CHOSEN FEW

The reality that ordinary people can be anointed by God to do His works and to serve as His mouthpieces is astounding when you consider how the anointing operated in the Old Testament. Under the old covenant, not every person who believed in the Lord was anointed or functioned as a prophet.

In those days, people who spoke for God or prophesied—like Noah, Abraham, Moses, Miriam, Deborah, Samuel, Isaiah, Ezekiel, and Malachi—were not average people, even though some may have started out that way. The prophets were a very specific group of people, men and women whom the Lord chose, called, and empowered. As I briefly mentioned earlier, prophets were considered by the rest of society to be unusual, special, unique—maybe even elite. They were considered extraordinary because they talked to God and conveyed to others what He was saying. They could sense God when no one else could.

Prophets saw things that no one else was seeing, heard things that no one else was hearing, and experienced things that no one else was experiencing. Moses, for instance, spoke to God through the burning bush (see Exodus 3:1–6), and he also was given the privilege of seeing God's "*back*" (see Exodus 33:18–23), which set him apart from others. Ezekiel saw visions of God's heavenly throne, and that set him apart. (See, for example, Ezekiel 1:25–28; 10:1–6.)

In ancient Jewish society, prophets were held in high esteem because of their position in the Spirit. When the average person wanted to know what God was saying or doing, they had to go to godly people who were called "seers" and inquire of them. The average Old Testament believer could only dream of a day when the anointed activities about which Isaiah spoke in Isaiah 61 would be possible for them, as they were for Jesus the Messiah, through the power of the Spirit. (See John 14:12.) It was only through Jesus Christ and the outpouring of His Spirit that such anointing became possible for every believer.

A NEW PROPHET

God is always looking for men and women through whom He can work. For a long time, He worked through a chosen few. But that method began to shift when Jesus arrived on the scene.

Jesus was not born at a Ritz-Carlton or Waldorf Astoria hotel. At birth, He was not clothed with baby blankets monogrammed with a Louis Vuitton label. Instead, He was wrapped in swaddling clothes and placed in a lowly manger. And He was born to a young, unknown virgin who had been overshadowed by God's Holy Spirit, enabling her to conceive the Son of God. Jesus's earthly father, Joseph, was a carpenter. Mary and Joseph were not people of means. They were humble, regular, normal people, and yet they had been chosen by God to raise His Son Jesus.

Although there were divine signs at Jesus's birth indicating that He was extraordinary, His early life was apparently very quiet and ordinary. But, as Jesus grew older, it became clear that He was anything but ordinary. Indeed, by the time He was a youth, He was doing some very unusual things—things other children didn't normally do. For instance, He purposefully spent time at the temple in Jerusalem, listening to the teachers and asking them questions. At a very early age, He was showing an inclination toward spiritual realities. (See Luke 2:41–52.)

Then, when Jesus was thirty, something utterly amazing happened. After faithfully enduring temptation by the devil in the wilderness, the carpenter's Son received God's anointing: "*Jesus returned in the power of the Spirit to Galilee, and news of Him went out through all the surrounding region. And He taught in their synagogues, being glorified by all*" (Luke 4:14–15 NKJV). Luke records what happened next:

> *He came to Nazareth, where He had been brought up. And as His custom was, He went into the synagogue on the Sabbath day, and stood up to read.* (Luke 4:16 NKJV)

It was Jesus's custom to attend synagogue. At his home synagogue in Nazareth, most times, He had probably just sat and listened like everyone else. But this time was different.

> *And He was handed the book of the prophet Isaiah. And when He had opened the book, He found the place where it was written: "The Spirit of the LORD is upon Me, because He has anointed Me to preach the gospel to the poor; He has sent Me to heal the brokenhearted, to proclaim liberty to the captives and recovery of sight to the blind, to set at liberty those who are oppressed; to proclaim the acceptable year of the LORD." Then He closed the book, and gave it back to the attendant and sat*

> *down. And the eyes of all who were in the synagogue were fixed on Him. And He began to say to them, "Today this Scripture is fulfilled in your hearing."* (Luke 4:16–21 NKJV)

Recall how prophets were regarded by the people. They were generally held in very high esteem because they were not everyday believers. A prophet was chosen by God for a specific purpose. And yet, here was Jesus, who, until very recently, had lived an obscure life, taking the scroll of the prophet Isaiah and opening it to the exact spot that spoke about Him, His anointing, and His purpose.

The first words He spoke were both powerful and controversial to the natural mind: *"The Spirit of the LORD is upon Me."* Whoa! In order to fully appreciate that statement, you have to understand the mindset of the people He was addressing. Only a prophet could say what He was saying. Only a prophet could hear *from* God and then speak *for* God, relaying His message to the people.

Not just anybody could have taken hold of that prophecy and declared, "This is my reality." When Jesus began to speak in this way, at first, the people *"marveled at the gracious words which proceeded out of His mouth"* (Luke 4:22 NKJV). But when He revealed the sinful state of their hearts, He became offensive to their religious minds. What He was saying and who He claimed to be were more than many could accept, and the people at the synagogue even set about to kill Him right then and there. (See verses 23–30.)

But for those who might have ears to hear, what He was saying was earth-shattering in a positive way. It was an announcement of the arrival of the Messiah, and it heralded an open door for anyone who would believe in Jesus to be received by the heavenly Father and operate in His Spirit's anointing.

GOD IS ALWAYS LOOKING FOR MEN AND WOMEN THROUGH WHOM HE CAN WORK.

A NEW ERA

In Jesus's words from Luke 4, I find at least six revelations about what God's anointing accomplishes. The anointing gives you...

1. Power to minister salvation
2. Power to heal—emotionally and physically—those who are sick
3. Power to proclaim freedom for those who are oppressed
4. Power to open blind eyes so that vision—both spiritual and physical—is restored
5. Power to minister deliverance. Every demon or every evil thought or idea that is contrary to the Spirit of almighty God must listen and obey when you rebuke it according to the authority of Christ, releasing and setting free people who have been bound by it
6. Favor, favor, and more favor!

Again, at the synagogue in Nazareth, Jesus did something very shocking for His time. In front of everyone, He proclaimed, in essence, that He had been sent by God, was a prophet of God, and carried the very power of God. As the revelation unfolded among Jesus's followers, those who indeed had ears to hear came to know and understand that He was not just a prophet. He was also the very Son of the living God. In fact, He was God Himself.

Jesus was anointed for miracles, and when He was thirty, miracles began to occur in His life and ministry. He turned water into wine, opened blind eyes and deaf ears, and enabled the lame to walk again. (See, for example, John 2:1–12; Matthew 9:27–31; Mark 7:32–35; John 5:1–9.) Those who were infirm with all sorts of diseases and sicknesses received miracles. "Incurable" lepers were healed, something that seemed absolutely impossible in the natural. (See, for example, Luke 5:12–14.) Jesus even raised dead people back to life! (See Luke 7:11–17; 8:49–56; John 11:43–44.) How much more spectacular could it get?

But, again, such miracles were offensive to people who had a religious mindset. (See, for example, Luke 13:10–17.) Why? There may have been a number of reasons, including self-righteousness and self-justification. But they were also being introduced to concepts they had never imagined before. Jesus was taking the written words of the prophets and bringing them alive with demonstration. What were they to do with a Man like this?

In Acts 1, we find Luke's record of some of Jesus's last words and acts on earth:

> *And being assembled together with them* [His disciples], *He commanded them not to depart from Jerusalem, but to wait for the Promise of the Father, "which," He said, "you have heard from Me; for John truly baptized with water, but you shall be baptized with the Holy Spirit not many days from now." Therefore, when they had come together, they asked Him, saying, "Lord, will You at this time restore the kingdom to Israel?" And He said to them, "It is not for you to know times or seasons which the Father has put in His own authority. But you shall receive power when the Holy Spirit has come upon you; and you shall be witnesses to Me in Jerusalem, and in all Judea and Samaria, and to the end of the earth."* (Acts 1:4–8 NKJV)

Jesus had offended the people at Nazareth by reading from Isaiah 61 and likening Himself to one of those few, select people who could engage with the Spirit of God, who could hear God, who could see God, who could feel God, who could smell God, who could taste God, and who could walk with God.

Now, just before His ascension, Jesus was saying something that would have been even more offensive to many of the religious leaders and people. When the Holy Spirit came upon His followers in a unique way, for the first time in history, the spiritual atmosphere would shift. Something altogether different would occur in God's unfolding plan for the world. Jesus was saying to His followers, to those who loved Him, "You are about to enter into a new era of living. There is a greater blessing coming, a dynamic change. The power of God will be given to you, and that power will be demonstrated *in and through* you." The anointing (symbolized by the holy anointing oil), which, until then, had been reserved exclusively for priests, kings, and prophets, was now being released to the everyday follower of Jesus. The power of God would be demonstrated through average people by the anointing of the Spirit! That, my friend, includes you and me. Yes, this blessing is for us today!

OILY MIRACLE TONGUES

How does God's anointing manifest in our everyday lives? One of the tangible ways in which the anointing overflows in us is by the miracle of speaking in tongues. In his first letter to the Corinthians, Paul said, *"I thank my God I speak with tongues more than you all"* (1 Corinthians 14:18 NKJV). The gift of tongues is a spiritual endowment that God wants us to regularly use to benefit ourselves and others. As Spirit-filled believers, we should speak in tongues and not be ashamed of this gift as we move in supernatural power.

When we speak in tongues, we are speaking the mysteries of God, we are building ourselves up in the Lord (see 1 Corinthians 14:2, 4), and we are stirring up the realm of the Spirit. There are no limits to speaking in tongues; we should do it whenever and wherever the Spirit prompts us. When I am in church, I speak in tongues. When I'm out in public, I speak in tongues. When I am in my home, I speak in tongues. Sometimes, even while I'm asleep, I speak in tongues. There have been times when I have awoken from sleep because Janet was loudly praying in the Spirit beside me in bed. Although our physical bodies need sleep, our spirits never sleep!

Janet and I believe that speaking in tongues also provides great encouragement for other believers. When we speak in tongues, we "oil" the spiritual atmosphere and build supernatural realms for God's power to be demonstrated. That's why, on several occasions, we have gone into the studio and recorded many tracks on which we worship

God and speak in tongues. Those tracks with our heavenly languages are actually some of the most sought-after recordings we have ever made. To this day, they have been played millions of times.[28] I pray you will discover what an amazing blessing it is to receive the miracle oil through speaking in tongues, which not only builds us and others up but can also be a catalyst for other manifestations of the anointing.

A FRESH ANOINTING

In this day and hour, we must hold fast to what we know to be true about the anointing from both Scripture and the Spirit. We also need to trust God to give us ways to increase our understanding of the anointing and to disseminate revelation about the miracle oil to others. We are to give away what has been given to us. In so doing, we will see a bountiful spiritual harvest, more fruitfulness than ever before. I can sense a fresh anointing of the Holy Spirit right now!

Let's pray together:

> Father, let Your miracle anointing come upon my life today in a whole new way. Thank You for anointing me to do the works You have planned for me to do. Empower me to accomplish what I could not otherwise accomplish. I am Your servant. I ask You to fill me to overflowing with Your Spirit. In Jesus's name, amen!

AS YOU CONTINUE TO READ THIS BOOK, IT IS MY PRAYER THAT YOU WILL CAPTURE THE ESSENCE OF GOD'S MIRACLE OIL IN YOUR SPIRIT, UNDERSTANDING THAT THERE IS MUCH DIVERSITY IN THE OUTPOURING OF GOD'S SPIRIT. MAY YOUR LIFE BE FILLED TO OVERFLOWING WITH *THE MIRACLE OF THE OIL*.

---

28. One of these recordings is our *Prayer Power* album, which is available to download or stream from online platforms.

14

MIRACLE ANOINTING MULTIPLIED!

"And they were all filled [that is, diffused throughout their being] with the Holy Spirit and began to speak in other tongues (different languages), as the Spirit was giving them the ability to speak out [clearly and appropriately]."
—Acts 2:4

The Spirit has always manifested in many unusual ways as Janet and I have ministered. Some years ago, when we hosted ministry meetings in Palm Springs, California, there was a young boy who attended the meetings with his grandmother. His name was Thomas, and although I haven't seen him for many years now, I have never forgotten him.

Thomas was just a child, yet he had great passion for the things of God. As I would minister, he would sit intently in his chair, seemingly soaking up each and every word that came from my lips.

He especially loved to hear the miracle testimonies as I shared stories about God's glory touching people. He always watched with wide-eyed amazement as signs and wonders began manifesting in extraordinary ways during the meetings.

Thomas's spiritual hunger was undeniable. He was certainly not a "doubting Thomas." (See John 20:24–31.) Instead, he was a "believing Thomas." His faith was pure, beautiful, and contagious.

On many occasions, as I would speak about God's anointing, a supernatural oil, such as I have described previously, would begin to form in the palms of Thomas's little open hands. He never sought attention or asked to be recognized. When the Spirit moved upon him in this way, he simply sat in his seat covered by a holy presence. I recognized this special manifestation occurring in Thomas's life, and I would often invite him to step out of his seat and stand with me to minister to the sick. Wonderful healings occurred in the meetings as many people were set free from long-standing illnesses they had been battling.

Many times, at such meetings, I have seen a supernatural transference of anointing happen wherever there is a spiritual "pull" from people. Those who have a great desire for God and His ways will receive the same kind of anointing that the leaders of the meetings have. Such occurrences seem to be a fulfillment of this statement by Jesus:

> *Blessed [joyful, nourished by God's goodness] are those who hunger and thirst for righteousness [those who actively seek right standing with God], for they will be [completely] satisfied.* (Matthew 5:6)

Hunger and desire can place a demand upon any type of anointing. Spiritual impartation happens when God's people seek the Lord, embrace the Spirit's challenge to willingly be stretched, and gracefully receive the anointing through a posture of faith. This is what happened for Thomas. That same miracle oil is available to you today. Are you ready to step into the anointing? As I wrote earlier, we should not be surprised if we begin to see various supernatural manifestations, such as tiny, diamond-like sparkles appearing on the palms of our hands, which sometimes transform into glistening miracle oil. These are some signs of the Spirit's anointing. Take a look at your hands even now and give the Spirit permission to work through you. You may see this manifestation in the spiritual realms, or you may see it physically happening. But however you see it, embrace it and follow God's guidance.

SET ON FIRE

The second chapter of Acts describes the events on the day of Pentecost when the Holy Spirit was poured out on Jesus's followers. Luke records that the believers were gathered together when something extraordinary happened.

> *Suddenly a sound came from heaven like a rushing violent wind, and it filled the whole house where they were sitting. There appeared to them tongues resembling fire, which were being distributed [among them], and they rested on each one of them [as each person received the Holy Spirit]. And they were all filled [that is, diffused throughout their being] with the Holy Spirit and began to speak in other tongues (different languages), as the Spirit was giving them the ability to speak out [clearly and appropriately].* (Acts 2:2–4)

Notice that Luke said these events happened *"suddenly."* If the believers were not prepared at that time, it was too late for them to get ready. The Spirit's outpouring had arrived. Even though they didn't know exactly what form the *"power from on high"* (Luke 24:49) would take, they couldn't say, "But no one told me it was coming." Jesus had told them to wait for *"the Promise of My Father"* (verse 49). Now they were in the process of receiving the Spirit. The rushing, mighty wind was there. The divided tongues of fire were there. Suddenly, *"they were all filled with the Holy Spirit and began to speak with other tongues, as the Spirit gave them utterance"* (Acts 2:4 NKJV).

We understand from the Scriptures that oil is symbolic of the power, the movement, and the presence of the Spirit. We might therefore visualize anointing oil being poured upon these early believers, beginning to soak them externally, and also welling up from within them. They were being filled with the Holy Spirit. They were being filled with *Someone*. That was a miracle of the holy oil!

Why, throughout these pages, have I so often referred to the "miracle oil," even titling this book *The Miracle of the Oil*? A miracle is something that cannot be explained through human logic or natural means. It defies the laws of nature. Miracles show us that there is a higher power, and we know that almighty God is moving and demonstrating His purposes and abilities. On the day of Pentecost, He was doing so through the humble followers of Jesus.

In Psalm 104:15, the psalmist wrote, *"So that he may make his face glisten with oil."* The spiritual concept is of God's anointing shining upon our faces. Without the miracle oil, we cannot have the light of God, and therefore our understanding of spiritual matters will be very basic. Yet, at Pentecost, when the Holy Spirit began to shine on and fill the people of God, they lit up. And miracle oil is given to us today so that we, too, can shine for Jesus, having been illuminated by His Spirit.

The light the believers received that day was not a small light. It was powerful light. These disciples of Jesus were set on fire, and they couldn't stop talking about what God had done—and was continuing to do—through Jesus Christ. The same will happen to you. When the Holy Spirit is poured out on you and in you, and you are lit on fire for the Lord, you will not be able to stop talking about what God has done in you, through you, for you, and around you.

> ***WHEN THE HOLY SPIRIT IS POURED OUT ON YOU AND IN YOU, AND YOU ARE LIT ON FIRE FOR THE LORD, YOU WILL NOT BE ABLE TO STOP TALKING ABOUT WHAT GOD HAS DONE IN YOU, THROUGH YOU, FOR YOU, AND AROUND YOU.***

AN OPEN INVITATION

The book of Acts records that, following this initial outpouring of the Holy Spirit at Pentecost, Peter stood up, took hold of the ancient prophetic words of Joel, and pulled those words into his present-day reality. "This," he essentially said, "is the very thing that was spoken of by the prophet Joel," and then he quoted the prophet:

> *"And it shall be in the last days," says God, "that I will pour out My Spirit upon all mankind; and your sons and your daughters shall prophesy, and your young men shall see [divinely prompted] visions, and your old men shall dream [divinely prompted] dreams; even on My bond-servants, both men and women, I will in those days pour out My Spirit and they shall prophesy."* (Acts 2:17–18)

Remember, Joel was one of the select few in Old Testament times through whom God released a prophetic word. What was God saying through Joel? He was saying, "You are *all* now invited to the outpouring. You are *all* invited to receive the oil." Hallelujah!

God said He would pour out His Spirit upon *"all mankind,"* and then He specified some of those who would receive. *"Your sons and your daughters"* would not only be filled with the Spirit, but they would *"prophesy." "Your young men shall see [divinely prompted] visions, and your old men shall dream [divinely prompted] dreams."* Since God mentioned both the young and the old, this effectively included all people. He also mentioned His *"bond-servants, both men and women"* and promised to pour out His Spirit upon them as well. They, too, would prophesy.

I want you to notice something here: sons and daughters, young men, old men, men and women, and even servants would receive the outpouring of the Spirit and become prophetic voices for God. Suddenly, a whole realm of spiritual possibilities was opening to all people!

Now everyone had the opportunity to spiritually see, hear, sense, smell, and taste the presence and working of the Spirit, and everyone could prophesy. When the Holy Spirit was released on the day of Pentecost, the people of God suddenly found their freedom. They were liberated so that they no longer had to depend on another person to hear from God and receive from Him. Now they could assemble corporately as the body of Christ, united in the Spirit, and receive the Spirit's outpouring. What could be more wonderful?

RIVERS OF OIL

This means that every believer now has access to the oil of God's Spirit, or the anointing. In a natural sense, oil is a precious and necessary commodity. But no oil on earth could be as precious and necessary as the oil of the Holy Spirit.

As I write this chapter, the world is experiencing an "oil war." There are oil shortages, with conflicts over the production, distribution, and availability of oil. Similarly, in the spiritual realms, we are waging war against the principalities of darkness that would try to block the spiritual blessings of God's miracle oil from coming to us. But God is equipping us in mighty ways and is pouring out His anointing upon us.

NO OIL ON EARTH COULD BE AS PRECIOUS, VALUABLE, AND NECESSARY AS THE OIL OF THE HOLY SPIRIT.

I became assured of this truth one night not long ago when I was on an airplane thirty-five thousand miles in the air above Oklahoma. Just before the plane began its descent into Tulsa, the Spirit of the Lord came upon me, and I began to prophesy out loud. My son, Lincoln, was sitting beside me, and when I began to speak, he turned to me and asked, "Dad, what are you doing?" I said, "I'm prophesying by the Spirit of God. He is giving me utterance." This is what the Lord said that night:

> "There shall be rivers of oil! There shall be a wave of oil that is bigger! There shall be a wave of oil that is stronger! This mighty wave will come with great blessing as I displace religious spirits and anoint the least likely among you. It will be much different than what you've seen in days gone by. This oil shall flow *for* unity, to bring forth the gathering of My chosen ones. And this oil shall increase *from* unity, as My people choose to walk hand in hand, side by side, anointed together in My Spirit.
>
> "For there shall be a greater anointing that rests upon My ministers that have stood in faith and contended for My promises to be fulfilled. Do not grow weary in doing what you've known to do, for My timings are perfect, and My will shall be accomplished through My faithful ones.
>
> "It may seem as though you've been in a wilderness season. Some have said, 'God, where are You in this place?' Others have spoken, saying, 'There are many churches, but this city is a spiritual desert.' But the Spirit of the Lord would say: 'It is not so! I am here, I am working in hearts, and I am preparing a resting place. No, this is not a

wilderness place; it is a chosen place. Know even now that this is not a desert place, for My Spirit is brooding over this city. This city is Mine,' declares the Lord! 'This state is Mine! This nation is Mine!'

"There shall be rivers of oil! Reservoirs of supernatural supply are being opened to you! It will be a testimony to many, and it will even be reported in the news! The floodgates of oil shall open, with an outpouring much greater than what you've seen in the past. It will be different in expression but of the same Spirit. You have known My presence in the past, so be discerning of My presence and the power of My anointing in this day even more. Be ready to drink of the oil. Be ready to swim in the rivers of My oil. Be ready to share My oil. For, in the days ahead, oh, even now, I am calling My people into proper position. The oil will come for transition from the old into the new. Divine alignment is necessary—not the plans of man but the plans of My Spirit being birthed in this city. Redesign, realign, revive, and restore! This is My heart for you," says the Lord.

LET THE OIL FLOW!

Praise God! We thank Him in advance for this great outpouring. We thank Him for those rivers of oil. We thank Him for the new oil, the fresh oil, that is coming; that fresh wave of the anointing of the Holy Spirit that is being poured out right now. Step into it! Receive of it! Drink from it! Swim in it! Enter into it! Allow the fresh anointing—the oil of the Lord, the oil of His presence, the oil of His power, the oil of His mercy, the oil of His healing, the oil of His sanctification, the oil of His holiness, the oil of His joy, the oil of His peace, the oil of His grace—to enter into you today.

Yes, let the oil flow! Stir yourself up in the Spirit. Pray in the Spirit, using your heavenly language, your spiritual tongue. Let

Deep call unto deep, Spirit unto spirit. (See Psalm 42:7.) Let the Spirit of God minister to your spirit. Let the flow of His anointing go deep within you! Be completely immersed in the Spirit.

A MOMENT OF TRANSITION

An oily presence of the Lord is flowing to you right now. It is the oil of breakthrough. This is a moment of transition for all who will receive it. You are moving into something deeper. You are going somewhere greater. God is bringing you into all that He has promised for your life. Lift your hands to heaven and receive the miracle oil of His presence.

Let the oil of heaven drip down upon you. Let rivers of oil begin to pour over you. Let the waves of God's oil begin to overtake you as you give yourself to the Holy Spirit's anointing. Let God do what He desires to do in the way He desires to do it, to His glory!

Let's pray together:

> Father, as Your miracle anointing is multiplied in these days, help me not to hold back for any reason but rather step fully into the rivers of Your glory. In Jesus's name, amen!

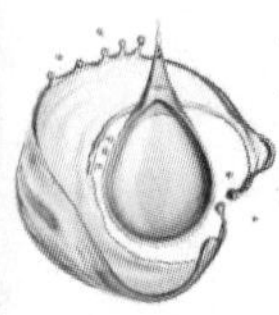

AS YOU CONCLUDE THIS BOOK, IT IS MY PRAYER THAT YOU WILL CAPTURE THE ESSENCE OF GOD'S MIRACLE OIL IN YOUR SPIRIT, UNDERSTANDING THAT THERE IS MUCH DIVERSITY IN THE OUTPOURING OF GOD'S SPIRIT. MAY YOUR LIFE BE FILLED TO OVERFLOWING WITH *THE MIRACLE OF THE OIL*.

MIRACLE OIL PRAYER

My friend, in the flow of the miracle oil, God meets all our needs. If you need healing, deliverance, or material provision today, let the oil of the Spirit flow *on* you, *in* you, and *through* you right now. Receive your miracle healing now. Receive your miracle deliverance now. Receive your miracle provision now. Lift up your hands and receive whatever it is that you need in the anointing of the Spirit. Don't wait—do it now!

There are unlimited provisions coming in a divine supply to you right now. Indebtedness is moving out, and an overflow of superabundance is moving in. The miracle of the oil is yours today. Receive it and allow it to bless your life in every way!

Let us pray:

> Lord, thank You for the miracle of the oil. The ways in which You are working among Your people are miraculous, and I give You the glory for them. I invite You, Holy Spirit, to anoint me in a new way today. Anoint my head, anoint my mind, anoint my heart, anoint my hands, anoint my feet, anoint everything that I have been entrusted with because Your anointing brings increase beyond imagination. That is the miracle of Your oil, and I am so thankful for it! Please use me to pass along to others the revelation of Your miracle oil in the anointing of Your Spirit. In Jesus's name, amen!

ABOUT THE AUTHOR

Joshua Mills is an internationally recognized, ordained minister of the gospel, as well as a recording artist, a keynote conference speaker, and the author of more than thirty books and spiritual training manuals. His recent books include *Creative Glory, 7 Divine Mysteries, Power Portals, Moving in Glory Realms, Seeing Angels,* and *Angelic Activations.* Joshua is well known for the supernatural atmosphere that he carries and for his unique insights into the glory realm and prophetic sound. Wherever Joshua ministers, the Word of God is confirmed by miraculous signs and wonders that testify of Jesus Christ. He is regarded as a spiritual forerunner in the body of Christ. For many years, he has helped people discover the life-shifting truths of salvation, healing, and deliverance for spirit, soul, and body. Joshua and his wife, Janet, cofounded International Glory Ministries and have ministered in over seventy-five nations on six continents. Featured together in several film documentaries and print articles, they have ministered to millions around the world through radio, television, and their weekly webcast, *Glory Bible Study.* They enjoy life with their three children, Lincoln, Liberty, and Legacy, and their puppy, Buttercup.